聖書を引用する世界の著名人

TOEFL iBT 形式で学ぶ英語と
グローバルリテラシー

Harris G. Ives　　上野　尚美
村上美保子　　小幡　幸和

開拓社

各章の **2** LISTENING SECTION で扱う英文の音声は，開拓社ホームページから
ダウンロードできます。

http://www.kaitakusha.co.jp/book/book.php?c=2313

は し が き

　最近,「グローバル」という言葉をよく耳にするようになりました。また,「グローバル人材の育成」とはどのような人材を育成するのかという議論も活発に行われています。本書では,「グローバル人材の育成」を下記のように定義しています。

豊かな教養と広い視野を持った人間を育成する教育。
アイデンティティーを確立しつつ
他者を正しく理解する能力を育む教育。
隣人愛を持って人と社会に奉仕し,
世界平和に貢献しようとする志を持った人間を育成する教育。

　冒頭に掲げた「豊かな教養」の「教養」には,さまざまな解釈があります。『広辞苑』では「一定の文化理想を体得」することと解説し,文部科学省では「ものの見方,考え方,価値観の総体」と説明しています。そのような教養を身に付けていると思われる著名人は,しばしば聖書から得られるメッセージをスピーチに引用しています。それはなぜでしょうか? 聖書の教えに現代の我々のものの見方や考え方に示唆するものがあるからではないでしょうか。グローバルに関連した用語として使われる "global literacy" は,通常「国際対話能力」と和訳されますが,他者を理解するための教養も要求される能力であるともいえます。

　本書では,著名な人物のスピーチ等で引用され,豊かな教養を持つ人が備えるべき教養の1分野として聖書をとらえ,それを "global literacy" の一部と定義し,みなさまにご紹介します。著名人を選択する際,できるだけ多様な職種・国籍から選ぶようにしました。

　また,「グローバル人材」になることを目標に英語学習に励む方々の中には,英語圏への留学を希望される方が多いだろうと推測しました。英語圏留学のために最も必要とされるのはTOEFL iBT (Test of English as a Foreign Language, Internet Based Testing) ですので,その対策にもなり得るように,TOEFL iBT の WRITING SECTION の Integrated（統合型）形式を採用することにしました。本書のレベルは,実用英語技能検定2級程度から1級程度を想定しています。我々は,この本を手に取ったみなさまが,"global literacy" として聖書を学び,同時に TOEFL iBT 対策ができることを願っています。

　最後に,BIBLE FOR GLOBAL LITERACY に関しては茨城キリスト教学園キリスト教センターの野口良哉チャプレン,英語本文に関しては茨城キリスト教大学文学部現代英語学科の David C. Yoshiba 教授,イラストに関しては児童教育学科の佃彰一郎教授,本書の企画段階から出版までお世話になりました開拓社の川田賢氏それぞれに対しても御礼申し上げます。

I. 本書の説明

「はしがき」にも書きました通り，本書は TOEFL iBT の WRITING SECTION の Integrated（統合型）形式を取り入れておりますが，TOEFL iBT 対策を主たる目的として書かれた本ではありません。したがって，TOEFL iBT 全般についての詳しい情報や対策は，他の本をご参照ください。ここでは，本書を効果的にお使いいただくために，TOEFL iBT の WRITING SECTION の Integrated（統合型）形式の説明と本書の使い方をご説明いたします。

まず，我々が TOEFL iBT の WRITING SECTION の Integrated（統合型）形式を採用した理由についてお話します。TOEFL iBT は，英語圏留学の際に使用されている英語力診断テストであり，その中でも WRITING SECTION の Integrated（統合型）形式を選んだのは，最も難易度が高いであろうと推定されるからです。一般的なテスト対策として，難易度が高い問題の対策をしておけば，他の形式の問題は比較的易しく感じられることと思います。なぜ難易度が高いのかといえば，Reading, Listening, Writing の 3 つのスキルを駆使して解答しなければならないからです。実際の Integrated（統合型）形式問題は，下記のような構成になっています。

1. 300 語程度の英文（Passage）を 3 分で読む。 (Reading)
2. 300 語程度の長さの英語（Lecture）を約 2 分間で聞く。 (Listening)
3. 150 語〜225 程度の長さで，1 に関連づけながら英語で，2 の要約文を書く。

(Writing)

この構成をご覧になっていただけばおわかりの通り，2 の英語を聞きとれなければ 3 の要約はできませんし，1 に関連づけて英文を書くこともできません。つまり，3 つのスキルが身についていなければ解答できない問題になっているため，他の英語力診断テストの問題形式よりも難易度が高いと判断いたしました。

本書では，聖書を引用した著名人およびその引用された聖書の言葉に焦点をあてており，形式も TOEFL iBT に準じています。つまり，本書の TOEFL iBT 形式の問題を解くことで，同テストの対策になり，我々が "global literacy" の一部であると定義づけた「聖書」についても学ぶことができるのです。

II. 本書の構成・使い方

1. READING SECTION

正確に時間を測り，指定された時間内で，Notes を参照せずに英文を読んでください。必要であると思われる箇所は，メモを取っても構いません。実際のテストでも，メモをとることは許可されています。

英文のレベルは，3 つに分かれています。初級（Elementary level: 英検 2 級レベル），

中級（Intermediate level: 英検準 1 級レベル），上級（Advanced level: 英検 1 級レベル）です。

2. **LISTENING SECTION**

READING SECTION で読んだ内容も踏まえて，LECTURE を聴きながらメモをとってください。

3. **QUESTION（SUMMARY）**

READING SECTION で読んだ内容と LISTENING SECTION で聞いた内容を要約してください。Summary を書く時間も指定されていますので，これも時間を正確に測って要約しましょう。模範解答を提示してありますので，自分で書いた Summary と比較してみてください。

4. **LECTURE TRANSCRIPT**

LISTENING SECTION で聞き取れなかった箇所を，確認してみましょう。

5. **BIBLE FOR GLOBAL LITERACY**

READING SECTION で扱われた聖書からの引用について解説してあります。

6. **CULTURAL NOTES**

READING SECTION や LISTENING SECTION で扱われた内容について，文化的に関連している事柄を解説してあります。

7. **READING SECTION NOTES**

1 の READING SECTION の NOTES です。

8. **LECTURE NOTES**

2 の LISTENING SECTION の NOTES です。

9. **SUMMARY SAMPLE**

3 の質問の模範解答ですので，参考にしてください。

10. **CHRISTIANITY AROUND YOU**

身近にある聖書やキリスト教について，教養として知っておいた方がよい情報を英語で紹介しています。第 1 章〜第 2 章，第 4 章〜第 9 章，第 11 章，第 14 章〜第 17 章，第 19 章に掲載しています。

TABLE OF CONTENTS
目次：本書で扱った著名人とその情報一覧

	章	頁	人名	職業	国籍/出身	聖書の引用個所	文化説明
初級	1	8	**Justin Bieber** ジャスティン・ビーバー	歌手	カナダ	旧約聖書・詩編119:105	グラミー賞 アメリカ音楽賞
	2	13	**Bill Gates** ビル・ゲイツ	マイクロソフト創業者	アメリカ	新約聖書・ルカによる福音書12:48	銀のスプーン
	3	19	**Usain Bolt** ウサイン・ボルト	陸上選手	ジャマイカ	旧約聖書・詩編23:4	ジャマイカ
	4	24	**Sadako Ogata** 緒方貞子	国連難民高等弁務官	日本	旧約聖書・イザヤ書2:4	ルワンダ虐殺 難民
	5	29	**Jeremy Lin** ジェレミー・リン	バスケットボール選手	アメリカ	旧約聖書・箴言16:3	アメリカプロバスケットボール(NBA)
	6	34	**Manny Pacquiao** マニー・パッキャオ	ボクサー	フィリピン	旧約聖書・エレミヤ書9:23	ボクシングのランク
	7	39	**Truett. S. Cathy** トゥルエット・キャシー	米国ファストフード店創業者	アメリカ	旧約聖書・箴言22:1	里親 聖書地帯
	8	44	**Rich Froning** リッチ・フロニング	クロスフィット選手	アメリカ	旧約聖書・エレミヤ書29:11	クロスフィット
中級	9	50	**Rikako Ikee** 池江璃花子	水泳選手	日本	新約聖書・コリントの信徒への手紙一10:13	白血病
	10	55	**Mariah Carey** マライア・キャリー	歌手	アメリカ	新約聖書・ヨハネによる福音書8:7	人種の多様性 サマー・キャンプ
	11	61	**Neymar** ネイマール	サッカー選手	ブラジル	旧約聖書・イザヤ書54:17	ブラジルのサッカー
	12	66	**J. K. Rowling** J. K. ローリング	作家	イギリス	新約聖書・マタイによる福音書16:26	チャリティー(慈善)
	13	71	**Chadwick Boseman** チャドウィック・ボーズマン	俳優	アメリカ	新約聖書・コリントの信徒への手紙一3:6	マーベル・エンターテイメント
	14	76	**Tomihiro Hoshino** 星野富弘	詩画作者	日本	新約聖書・マタイによる福音書11:28	富弘美術館
	15	81	**Maria Callas** マリア・カラス	オペラ歌手	ギリシャ/アメリカ	新約聖書・マタイによる福音書6:24	オペラ

16	87	**Kent Brantly** ケント・ブラントリー	医師（エボラ）	アメリカ	旧約聖書・ダニエル書 3:17-18	エボラ出血熱
17	93	**Bennet Omalu** ベネット・オマル	スポーツ医学者	ナイジェリア	新約聖書・エフェソの信徒への手紙 4:22, 24	アメリカンフットボール
18	98	**Pharrell Williams** ファレル・ウィリアムス	歌手	アメリカ	新約聖書・コリントの信徒への手紙一 13:11	ファッションリーダードレスコード
19	103	**Prince William** ウィリアム王子	英国王室メンバー	イギリス	新約聖書・コリントの信徒への手紙一 13:4-5	ギャップ・イヤー
20	109	**Mahatma Gandhi** マハトマ・ガンディー	政治家	インド	新約聖書・マタイによる福音書 5:39	インドの宗教
21	115	**Dalai Lama** ダライ・ラマ	チベット仏教指導者	チベット	新約聖書・マルコによる福音書 3:33-35	チベット仏教
22	121	**Victor Frankl** ヴィクトール・E・フランクル	精神科医	オーストリア	旧約聖書・詩編 118:5	ホロコースト
23	127	**Ted Turner** テッド・ターナー	CNN 創業者	アメリカ	新約聖書・使徒言行録 20:35	アメリカ・TVニュース番組 (CNN)
24	132	**Eddie Redmayne** エディ・レッドメイン	俳優	イギリス	旧約聖書・コヘレトの言葉 3:1-2, 4, 11	スティーブン・ホーキンズ博士
25	138	**Wangari Maathai** ワンガリ・マータイ	環境活動家	ケニア	新約聖書・使徒言行録 3:6	もったいない (環境 3R)
26	144	**Shigeaki Hinohara** 日野原重明	医師	日本	新約聖書・ヤコブの手紙 1:12	音楽療法
27	150	**Thabo Mbeki** タボ・ムベキ	政治家	南アフリカ	旧約聖書・箴言 3:27-28	アパルトヘイト
28	156	**David Suchet** デイビッド・スーシェ	俳優	イギリス	新約聖書・マルコによる福音書 6:31	名探偵エルキュール・ポワロ
29	162	**Rick Warren** リック・ウォーレン	牧師	アメリカ	新約聖書・ローマの信徒への手紙 12:2	ダニエル・プランベジタリアン
30	168	**Buzz Aldrin** バズ・オルドリン	宇宙飛行士	アメリカ	旧約聖書・詩編 8:4-5	アポロ 11 号

上級

Chapter 1 / *Justin Bieber*

1 READING SECTION

Read the following passage for 3 minutes.

Born in Canada in 1994, Justin Bieber is a global music idol. His Twitter account has over 110 million followers, and his Instagram has more than 140 million followers. His YouTube videos have been played more than 20 billion times. His famous songs include *What Do you Mean?*, *Love Yourself*, and *Sorry*. 5

Bieber is handsome, and his muscular body is covered with tattoos. Most recently, he attended the Formula One Racing event in Singapore. He wore a tank top. Many people noticed the words tattooed on his back: "Your word is a lamp for my feet, a light on my path." This is a quotation from the Book of Psalms in the Bible. 10

The quotation represents life as a journey. The traveler is walking at night. He carries a lamp so that he can see the way more clearly. The light assures the traveler that he is on the right path. It keeps him from stumbling or tripping on rocks, or falling into holes. The words "falling" and "stumbling" are metaphors for mistakes we make 15 in our lives. The above quotation implies that we can avoid making mistakes by following a "light." That light helps us to make the best decisions. Do you have such a light in your life?

2 LISTENING SECTION

Listen to a lecture on the topic you just read about.　

3 QUESTION (SUMMARY)

Summarize the points made in the lecture, being sure to explain how the Reading Section deepens the understanding of the lecture passage (100 to 125 words).　You have 20 minutes to plan and write your response.

4 LECTURE TRANSCRIPT

When Justin Bieber was a child, his mother posted videos of him singing on YouTube.　Those videos became very popular.　American musicians such as L.A. Reid and Usher saw Bieber's performances and promoted his career. *Forbes* magazine has ranked Bieber among "The Top Ten Most Powerful Celebrities in the World" for the years 2011, 2012, and 2013.　He has been honored at the Grammy Awards, as well as the American Music Awards.

As Justin Bieber became a world-class pop star, the media reported a series of his misbehaviors.　For example, Bieber threw eggs at his neighbor's house.　He attacked reporters.　He was even arrested for driving under the influence of alcohol and drugs.　Bieber admitted he made silly mistakes. So, he said, "I wanna be a man that learns from [those mistakes] and grows from them."　He talks about God's forgiveness in one of his music videos. He gets such ideas by reading the Bible.

Justin Bieber is also known for his charity.　He has given large amounts of money for disaster relief in the Philippines.　His organization, "Schools 4 All," builds campuses in underdeveloped countries.　His talent, good looks, and his lifestyle guarantee he'll be in the headlines for many years.

"Your word is a lamp for my feet, a light on my path." (Psalm 119:105 [NIV])

「あなたの御言葉は，わたしの道の光　わたしの歩みを照らす灯。」（詩編 119 編 105 節）

　ジャスティン・ビーバーの右肩にタトゥーとして刻まれているこの言葉は，旧約聖書中の『詩編』（『詩篇』）にある一節です。旧約聖書は 39 の書の集まりなのですが，『詩編』はその中の一つの書です。『詩編』は複数の人の手によって記された 150 もの詩が詩集として編纂されたもので，古代イスラエル民族の信仰の表明，祈りの言葉とも言えるものです。

　ここで "Your word"「あなたの御言葉」とあるのは，「神の言葉」・「神の語る言葉」を指します。キリスト教は啓示宗教であり，神が人間に語る言葉が重要視されます。それは，目に見えない神の意志や思いが「ことば」を通して人に伝えられるからに他なりません。聖書によれば，神の言葉は人間を慰め励ますと同時に，人間よりも大きな存在である神の視点からものごとの善悪を示すものです。上記の詩の作者は，人生の歩みにおいて「神の言葉」がいかに大切であるかを，暗闇を照らす光という隠喩（メタファー）で詩的に表現しています。この一節はキリスト教世界では極めてよく知られた言葉で，ジャスティン・ビーバーのタトゥー以外にも英語の文章の様々な所で目にすることがあるでしょう。

　ちなみに，英語では，書（詩集）としての『詩編』は "Psalms" または "The Book of Psalms"，一つ一つの「詩」は "psalm" と表記されます。そして，大文字の "P" から始まることで書としての『詩編』を指す場合には "s" が付いていても単数扱いになります。（例 "Psalms is a collection of poems." 〔『詩編』は詩の集まりである〕）

6 CULTURAL NOTES

　ジャスティン・ビーバーが受賞しているグラミー賞とアメリカ音楽賞は，どちらもアメリカの音楽業界で優れた歌手や楽曲に対して贈られる権威のある賞です。

　グラミー賞は，レコード会社などによって組織されている非営利団体 NARAS（全米録音芸術科学アカデミー）が主宰し，1958 年度が第 1 回で，最優秀レコード，最優秀アルバム，最優秀歌曲，最優秀男性歌手，最優秀女性歌手，クラシックからもオーケストラ，器楽，声楽など 6 部門と，合計 28 の賞が与えられました。回を追うごとに部門数が増え，現在では，40 以上の賞が出されるようになっています。（『世界大百科事典 第 2 版』）

　一方，アメリカ音楽賞は，1973 年に創設された音楽に関する賞で，グラミー賞ではエンターテインメント産業の業界人によって受賞者が選ばれますが，アメリカ音楽賞では，ファンの投票で選ばれます。したがって，両者を授賞したジャスティン・ビーバーは，若いながらも，その音楽・歌唱の質と人気の両方で広く認められたことになります。

7 READING SECTION NOTES

l. 1.　idol　アイドル

l.13.　keep from　（～すること）を避ける

l.14.　stumble　よろける，つまずく

l.14.　trip　つまずく，つまずいて倒れる

l.16.　imply　暗示する

8 LECTURE NOTES

l. 5.　celebrity　有名人

l.11.　wanna=want to の省略形。カジュアルな表現

l.17.　guarantee 保証する

The lecture outlines the life of Justin Bieber. He is a popular singer whom an American magazine ranks as one of the Top Ten Most Powerful Celebrities in the World. Among his songs are *What do you mean?* and *Love Yourself*. Although Bieber is loved among many young people, he has done some bad things. For example, he threw eggs at his neighbor's house. He has also been arrested for driving while drunk. Despite these bad actions, he has tried to be a better person. As the Reading Section implies, Bieber wants to change himself. He has tattooed his body with a Bible verse which talks about following a "light."

10 CHRISTIANITY AROUND YOU

<Confession 告解，罪の告白>

Several times in his life and in his music, Justin Bieber has admitted faults, asked for forgiveness, and expressed a determination to be a better man. In his song, *Sorry*, he speaks to a lover: "Oh, is it too late now to say sorry? Yeah, I know I let you down." Those ideas are the basis of confession, a prominent Christian ideal. He expresses being sorry for the bad decisions of his life. As a member of the Hillsong Church, Bieber wrote a long essay about his sorrow over past misbehavior. He is not alone in confessing. Sometimes in Protestant churches, people stand up and ask for forgiveness. Many movies have scenes of Roman Catholic-style confession: a man or woman enters a small, dark, booth and speaks to a priest about misbehavior. The September 2019 issue of *Newsweek* magazine says that Bieber has become a "changed man" because of the confession he posted on Instagram.

Chapter 2 / *Bill Gates*

1 READING SECTION

Read the following passage for 3 minutes.

Recognized as the main founder of Microsoft Corporation, Bill Gates decided with his wife to focus on giving their money away. The couple travels extensively to developing regions of the world. They seek ways to help poor, disadvantaged people. They are particularly interested in global health. They want to relieve people suffering 5 from hunger and from tropical diseases. Further, they promote the education of young girls and women. In his 2007 speech at Harvard University, he used these words to express his reason for charity: "From those to whom much is given, much is expected."

These are similar to words in the Bible (Luke 12:48). Jesus was 10 teaching his students that they have an obligation to help others. The idea is that people who have much money and access to the good things in life should share with others. Bill Gates is aware that he enjoys many privileges because of his high intelligence and his fortune. Various researchers debate who is the richest man in the world, 15 and Bill Gates' name is frequently included among the very top people. He is not concerned about getting more money. He is not only rich in money, he is rich in friendships.

2 LISTENING SECTION

Listen to a lecture on the topic you just read about.

3 QUESTION (SUMMARY)

Summarize the points made in the lecture, being sure to explain how the Reading Section deepens the understanding of the lecture passage (100 to 125 words). You have 20 minutes to plan and write your response.

4 LECTURE TRANSCRIPT

Some Americans might say, "Bill Gates was born with a silver spoon in his mouth." That idiom simply means that a person was born into a wealthy family and enjoyed many advantages. Gates was born in 1955, in Seattle, Washington. His father was an important lawyer, and his mother was on the board of a bank. More importantly, Gates was obviously a very intelligent child. The administrators at his private middle school hired Gates and three friends to write special computer programs. Gates had the responsibility of designing a program for registering students in classes. Always clever, he placed himself in a class which had many beautiful girls. Not only did the school provide computers for Gates and friends to use, the young geniuses were also paid for their work.

He scored very high on the college entrance examination, earning a place at Harvard University in 1973. He dropped out of college after two years. Although no longer a student, he worked with a famous computer scientist and published an academic paper. He and his partner, Paul Allen, launched Microsoft Corporation in 1975, which became the world's largest computer software company.

5 BIBLE FOR GLOBAL LITERACY

"... From everyone who has been given much, much will be demanded ..." (Luke 12:48 [NIV])

「... すべて多く与えられた者は，多く求められ，多く任された者は，更に多く要求される。」（ルカによる福音書 12 章 48 節）

　これは，新約聖書にあるイエス・キリストの言葉の一つです。お金であれ能力であれ，より多くを与えられた者の責任について教えているこの言葉は，とりわけアメリカ社会では広く一般に知られた言葉となっています。

　イエス・キリストは，この言葉に合わせて，ある「たとえ話」を語っています。それは，主人に財産管理を任された召使いについての話でした。この話によれば，召使いは多くの財産を扱っていますが，その財産は自分の力で得たものでも，自分の好き勝手に使って良いものでもありません。その財産の本来の持ち主である主人は，良いことのためにその財産を使って欲しいと願って，召使いに財産の運用を委ねたのでした。

　聖書によれば，この話の主人とは目に見えない神，そして召使いとは一人一人の人間であるとされます。つまり，人間が「持っているもの」は，究極的には神から「与えられたもの（賜物）」であり，神が望む良いことのために用いられるべきという教えがここにあります。「与えられたもの」は，お金とは限りません。例えば，能力があります。能力とは，何も勉強や仕事ができることだけではありません。努力できること，人を笑わせられること，優しい言葉を投げかけられること，等も能力の一つでしょう。そして，どんな能力にせよ，それを与えられている人は，それらを良いことのため，つまり利己的な目的でなく他者のために用いる責任があるというのがこの言葉の意味なのです。より多くを持つことを否定するのではなく，何であれ自分が持つものを他者のために用いる責任を語るのがこの言葉です。ビル・ゲイツは，まさにそれを実践しようとしているのではないでしょうか。

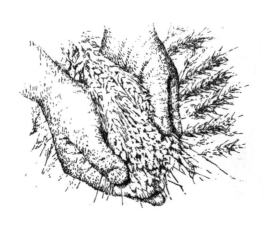

6 CULTURAL NOTES

　本章の，born with a silver spoon in one's mouth（裕福な家に生まれた）の直訳は，「銀のスプーンをくわえて生まれた」です。もちろん比喩ですが，なぜダイヤの指輪とか金の冠とかではなく，銀のスプーンなのでしょうか。古来，銀は魔を退ける力があると考えられてきた金属です。これは強い酸や硫黄など人体に有害な物質に即座に反応して黒く変色することから発想されたと考えられます。この作用を利用して，王侯貴族の毒見用の食具に利用されたことからも，銀が深く信頼されてきた歴史がわかります。中世ヨーロッパでは，貴金属製の食具は大変貴重で，王侯貴族が代々財産として継承するものでした。16 ～ 17 世紀，イギリスでは「使徒のスプーン」という贈り物が流行するようになります。これは，スプーンの柄にキリストの十二使徒の一人をかたどった彫刻が施されたもので，洗礼を受けた子どもの名付け親がその子のクリスチャンネームにちなんだ守護聖人を彫って記念に贈る習わしです。当時のイギリスは大航海時代の波に乗って世界中の富が集まる場所でした。豊かな階級は，蓄財性の高い銀の食器・食具を使用していました。これが，銀のスプーンのことわざのもととなり，洗礼時の贈り物の風習とともに現代へと伝えられました。現在でも，食べ物に苦労することなく，経済的な安定と幸せが続くように願って，銀のスプーンが出産祝いで贈られることがあります。(http://www.silver-babyspoon.com/)

7 READING SECTION NOTES

l. 3.　developing regions　開発途上地域

l. 4.　disadvantaged people　（経済的・社会的に）恵まれない人々

l. 8.　charity　慈善行為

l.11.　obligation　義務

l.14.　privilege　特権

8 LECTURE NOTES

l. 3.　enjoy many advantages　多くの利益を享受する

l. 4.　on the board　取締役に就いて

l.15.　launch　立ち上げる

9 SUMMARY SAMPLE

The Lecture states that Bill Gates was an intelligent student. Administrators of his middle school recognized his talent. They provided him and his three friends with computers and asked them to design computer programs. He and his friends were paid for their work. Later, Gates entered Harvard University. Although he dropped out after two years, he did become the founder of Microsoft Corporation. The Reading Section says, in his 2007 speech at Harvard, Gates used words from the Bible. He said we should use our wealth and talents to help other people. He, himself, travels with his wife looking for ways to help underprivileged people.

10 CHRISTIANITY AROUND YOU

<Charity 善意, チャリティー>

Bill Gates has been cautious about mentioning God in his public speeches although he is beginning to refer to spiritual principles. In his Harvard commencement speech, he acknowledged the responsibility of rich people to help others. His wife, Melinda, is a Roman Catholic, though she has some disagreement with the religion. Both of them believe that true charity is more than just dropping coins into the hands of a beggar. They believe in funding projects that improve health and create opportunities for people to become creative. Both are interested in women's education. Melinda's new book, *The Moment of Lift: How Empowering Women Changes the World*, expresses her determination to help women achieve their rights. For her, and for her husband, charity involves education. She says that her Catholic school education had taught her the values of social justice. Today, she and her husband are not satisfied with merely giving money. They invest in schools and programs which promote respect for all people, particularly women. That is the essence of Christian charity: helping people feel good about themselves. Many times people believe that they are charitable because they have given small change to homeless people. More than being church attendees, Bill and Melinda Gates are practitioners of Christian charity.

Chapter 3 / *Usain Bolt*

1 READING SECTION

Read the following passage for 3 minutes.

Born in a poor Jamaican village in 1986, Usain Bolt spent his early years without electricity and running water in his home. Having won nine Olympic medals in sprinting, Bolt constantly expresses his gratitude to God. In 2014 he suffered a hamstring injury. He was nervous about his future, but he continued his trust in God. Before winning the gold medal in the 2015 World Championship, he tweeted Psalm 23:4. It reads, "Yea, though I walk through the valley of the shadow of death, I will fear no evil: for thou art with me." [5]

Anyone who has watched American movies has probably heard Psalm 23 read in funeral or wedding scenes. The idea of the psalm is that God protects the people who trust Him. Verse 4 presents the scene of someone walking through a valley in which all kinds of dangers lurk. Maybe there are dangerous animals, or maybe there are gun-holding enemies waiting to attack the innocent person. These frightening movie images are comparable to the more realistic "dangers" such as contracting cancer, or losing a job, or being abandoned by a lover. According to the psalm, God is aware of all suffering and will lead the good person to relief. [10] [15]

2 LISTENING SECTION

Listen to a lecture on the topic you just read about.

3 QUESTION (SUMMARY)

Summarize the points made in the lecture, being sure to explain how the Reading Section deepens the understanding of the lecture passage (100 to 125 words). You have 20 minutes to plan and write your response.

4 LECTURE TRANSCRIPT

Born in 1986, Usain Bolt is a retired sprinter from Jamaica. He is noted for his religious gestures after each race. At the start of races, he often makes the *Sign of the Cross*. At the end of his many victories, he holds his index finger up to heaven in celebration. Occasionally, he tweets a Bible verse. In his opinion, he must thank God for his success. He is a 5 world record holder in the 100 and 200 meters. Nine times he has won the Olympic gold medal. He has been honored as the IAAF World Athlete of the Year, the Track and Field Athlete of the Year, and the BBC Overseas Sports Personality of the Year. Usain Bolt's full name gives some insight into his family's religious background: Usain *St. Leo* Bolt! 10

Despite his religious gestures and his constant smiling, Bolt has been criticized by some people for being a braggart. Once, sportscasters criticized Bolt for slapping his chest after a successful race. They accused him of "showboating" (bragging about his talent). Bolt said, "I was not bragging ... I was happy." Having achieved success in the 2009 Berlin Olympics and 15 the 2016 Rio Olympics, Bolt has reason to be happy.

5 BIBLE FOR GLOBAL LITERACY

"Yea, though I walk through the valley of the shadow of death, I will fear no evil: for thou art with me ..." (Psalms 23:4 [KJV])

「死の陰の谷を行くときも　わたしは災いを恐れない。あなたがわたしと共にいてくださる。…」（詩編 23 編 4 節）

　上記の言葉が含まれる詩編 23 編は，『詩編』の中で，あるいは聖書全体で最も多く引用される言葉かもしれません（『詩編』については，１章の **BIBLE FOR GLOBAL LITERACY** を参照）。

　この詩においては，作者は自らのことを羊に例え，つねに自分を守っている神のことを羊飼いに例えています。上記 4 節の前には，神は「わたしを青草の原に休ませ，憩いの水のほとりに伴い…わたしを正しい道に導かれる」と記されています（詩編 23 編 2 節 − 3 節）。地中海世界において広く放牧されている羊には，放牧ならではの危険も伴います。それは狼などの外敵かもしれませんし，崖などの障壁かもしれません。「死の陰の谷」とは，そうしたあらゆる危険を表す比喩的表現です。そして，あらゆる危険から羊を守るのが羊飼いの役目なのです。

　READING SECTION にあるように，詩編 23 編はキリスト教の葬儀（告別式）や埋葬式（日本では納骨式）において牧師が朗読する定番の言葉になっています。この言葉によって，亡くなった人と，愛する人を失った人の両方が神に守られていることが確認されるのです。

6 CULTURAL NOTES

　ジャマイカは山や熱帯雨林，サンゴ礁のビーチといった緑豊かな自然を誇るカリブ海の島国です。イギリスの旧植民地で，イギリス連邦加盟国であるため公用語は英語です。ジャマイカの有名人には，ボブ・マーレイのようなミュージシャン（レゲエというジャマイカ発祥の音楽で知られています）やウサイン・ボルトのようなアスリートがいます。

　ウサイン・ボルトは，ジャマイカ出身の元陸上競技短距離選手で，2002年から2017年までの現役時代には数々の記録を樹立し，人類史上最速のスプリンターと評されました。100メートル，200メートルの世界記録保持者です。天に向かって弓矢を射るような，稲妻の形状に似たポーズをゴールした後にすることが多く，稲妻を意味する「ライトニング」をつけて，「ライトニング・ボルト」という愛称で呼ばれました。

7 READING SECTION NOTES

l. 1.　Jamaican　ジャマイカ島の
l. 3.　sprinting　短距離
l. 4.　hamstring　ハムストリング腱（大腿部後部にある筋肉群）
l.13.　lurk　潜在する
l.15.　comparable　相当する
l.16.　contract　病気にかかる
l.16.　abandon　捨てる

8 LECTURE NOTES

l. 1.　retired　引退した
l. 1.　noted　有名な
l. 3.　make the *Sign of the Cross*　十字を切る
l. 4.　index finger　人差し指
l. 4.　in celebration　祝って
l. 4.　occasionally　時々
l. 4.　tweet　ツイートする
l. 5.　verse　（聖書の）節
l. 7.　honor　高く評価する
l. 7.　IAAF (International Association of Athletics Federations)*　国際陸上競技連盟
　　　　*2019年に World Athletics に名称変更

l. 7.　athlete of the year　その年の最優秀運動選手

l. 8.　track and field　陸上競技

l. 9.　personality　人物

l. 9.　insight into　〜に対する洞察力

l.12.　braggart　自慢屋

l.13.　slap　平手でピシャリと打つ

l.13.　accuse　非難する

l.14.　showboat　派手なプレーをする

l.14.　brag　自慢する

9 SUMMARY SAMPLE

According to the Lecture, Usain Bolt is a retired Olympic sprinter. He has won medals in the sport. He performs religious gestures before and after races. He came from a very poor family in Jamaica. The religious background of his family is indicated by his complete name: Usain St. Leo Bolt. Even though he smiles and points his index finger to heaven, Bolt has been accused of pride. Once he slapped his chest after a victory. Some sportscasters interpreted that as an indication of his excessive pride. Bolt defended his action. He said that he was not bragging. He was only showing his happiness. The Reading Section gives one example of Bolt's faith in God: when he suffered a severe injury, he was very worried about his future in the sport. He got better. He attributes his recovery to God.

1 READING SECTION

Read the following passage for 3 minutes.

Sadako Ogata served the United Nations in several positions. She taught at both International Christian University and Sophia University. The Christian values she learned on those campuses prepared her for a career in solving conflicts and providing assistance to the needy. She traveled extensively to war-torn areas to provide relief to refugees and poor children. In a speech attended by President Karzai of Afghanistan, Ogata mentioned Japan's commitment to improving education in that area. A highly educated woman, Ogata was convinced that better schools and greater access for girls were essential for international understanding. She concluded that speech with a reference to Isaiah 2:4. "He (God) will judge between the nations, and will settle disputes for many peoples. They will beat their swords into plowshares ..." 5

10

The passage is a prediction of a happy time in the future. It contains an image of people converting their weapons into farm tools. It anticipates a Utopian future where former enemies will embrace each other as friends. Visitors to Ontario, Canada can see *The Swords into Plowshares Museum* where military tanks have been changed into snowplows. Sadako Ogata worked for that dream of peace. 15

2 LISTENING SECTION

Listen to a lecture on the topic you just read about.

3 QUESTION (SUMMARY)

Summarize the points made in the lecture, being sure to explain how the Reading Section deepens the understanding of the lecture passage (100 to 125 words). You have 20 minutes to plan and write your response.

4 LECTURE TRANSCRIPT

Sadako Ogata was one of the most internationally recognizable faces during the 1980s and 90s. She was a peace negotiator. She was born in Tokyo in 1927. She lived to be 92 years old and had served in various posts at the United Nations. Her academic record was impressive. She graduated from the University of the Sacred Heart in Tokyo. Later, she earned a Ph.D. in Political Science from the University of California, Berkeley. In Japan, she taught at Sophia University and at International Christian University.

Ogata was an adviser on international as well as domestic issues. She served on a special panel which recommended female succession to the imperial throne in Japan. Uppermost in her mind was according respect to all people, regardless of their social status.

At a special tribute to her in Tokyo in 2012, Prime Minister Yoshihiko Noda said that Ogata had enhanced international appreciation of Japan. Japan had just suffered the 2011 earthquake disaster, and the Prime Minster noted that many countries were quick to offer assistance. He said this great support was "not irrelevant to Mrs. Sadako Ogata's achievements."

"... They will beat their swords into plowshares ..." (Isaiah 2:4 [NIV])

「... 彼らは剣を打ち直して鋤とし ...」（イザヤ書 2 章 4 節）

『イザヤ書』は，旧約聖書の預言書部分の冒頭に配置される書で，新約聖書の中で引用されることも多い重要な書です。この書は分量が多く，時代背景的にも紀元前 8 世紀から紀元前 6 世紀の長きにわたります。内容的にも，神の民の腐敗に対する警告と裁き，そして神の民の挫折と絶望の後に来る回復の予告など多岐に及びます。また，ほとんどが詩文体で記され，比喩的表現に満ちているのがこの書です。

上記の言葉は，そんな『イザヤ書』の一節です。ここで描かれているのは，争いが止み，平和が訪れる「終わりの日」と呼ばれる世界（終末）についての幻（vision）です。その世界においては，人々は剣の鉄を火で打ち直して農具に変えるとされます。もはや武器を持つ必要がないからです。「終わりの日」の「終わり」（end）とは，時間の流れの最後という意味だけでなく，「目的・目標」とも解釈できます。

現代世界には，いまだに武器が満ちています。そんな現状を目の前にしても，武器で互いの命を奪い合うことが人間の究極の目的（end）ではないと信じ，いま自分が踏み出せる一歩を踏み出すこともできるはずです。元国連難民高等弁務官でキリスト教徒（カトリック）でもあった緒方貞子さんは，この聖書の言葉に示唆されている幻（vision）を見ていたのではないでしょうか。

6 CULTURAL NOTES

　難民は，戦争，民族紛争，政治的迫害，経済的困窮，自然災害などの理由によって居住区域を離れた人々を指します。緒方貞子氏は，難民支援を世界の国々に要請する国連難民高等弁務官という仕事をしていました。

　1994年にアフリカのルワンダで起こった民族紛争に端を発する虐殺では，約100日の間に，50万人とも100万人ともいわれる全国民の10〜20%が殺されたとされています。ルワンダ難民キャンプ支援として，緒方氏の要請を受けて日本政府はルワンダ難民支援の実施計画と関連する法令を閣議決定し，国際平和協力法に基づき，自衛隊ルワンダ難民救援派遣を行いました。

7 READING SECTION NOTES

l. 4.　needy　貧しい人々

l. 5.　extensively　広範囲に（わたって）

l. 5.　war-torn　戦乱の

l. 7.　Afghanistan　アフガニスタン（正式国名：the Islamic Republic of Afghanistan）

l. 7.　commitment　深い関与

l.15.　convert ... into~　…を〜に改造する

l.16.　Utopian　ユートピアの，理想郷の

l.16.　embrace　抱き合う，抱擁する

l.19.　snowplow　除雪車

8 LECTURE NOTES

l. 1.　recognizable　誰もが知る

l. 5.　University of the Sacred Heart　聖心女子大学

l. 9.　succession　継承者

l. 9.　imperial throne　皇位

l.10.　uppermost　真っ先に

l.10.　according　準じた

l.12.　tribute　賛辞

l.13.　enhance　高める

l.13.　appreciation　評価

l.16.　not irrelevant to　無関係ではない

Sadako Ogata worked for the United Nations and served in several different jobs having to do with relieving people who were suffering in war zones. As the Reading Section says, she was influenced by the Christian values of several institutions where she studied and taught. She was an educated woman who was influential in Japan and in the world. Abroad, she worked to bring relief to refugees. In Japan, she served on a committee which studied the possibility of a woman succeeding to the throne. She focused on insuring respect for all people. Prime Minister Noda said many countries were eager to help Japan after the 2011 earthquake because of their respect for Ogata.

10 CHRISTIANITY AROUND YOU

<Christian Universities キリスト教主義大学>

Throughout the world there are colleges and universities with religious backgrounds. Empress Emerita Michiko and Sadako Ogata are both graduates of the University of the Sacred Heart in Tokyo, a Catholic institution. Princesses Mako and Kako are graduates of International Christian University which has a very interesting background: Hisato Ichimada, a Buddhist, cooperated with Christians of different groups to build the school. Of the many well-known schools which have Christian backgrounds are Oxford University, England; Stanford University, USA; Sorbonne University, France; and Salamanca University, Spain. Such famous universities as Yale, Princeton, and Harvard were founded by Christians.

Chapter 5 / *Jeremy Lin*

1 READING SECTION

Read the following passage for 3 minutes.

Jeremy Lin is one of a few successful Asian-American players in the National Basketball Association of the United States, also known as the NBA. While playing for the New York Knicks in 2012, he scored 38 points in a game against the strong rival team, Los Angeles Lakers. His spectacular performance caused a national phenomenon known as [5] "Linsanity." People thought Lin's performance was "insanely" good —that's why, "Linsanity."

Behind Lin's success is his philosophy of life. In several of his writings, he quotes the following words: "Commit to the Lord whatever you do, and your plans will succeed." The words come from the [10] Book of Proverbs in the Bible (Proverbs 16:3). These words reflect what Lin believes.

In the above words, "committing to the Lord (or God)" means to be humble. We should not brag about our talents. We must realize that our talents are gifts from God, and we should be thankful for them. [15] Also, committing to the Lord means being honest. Success based on dishonest behaviors is meaningless. Finally, these words promise success to people who commit to God with humility and honesty. Such commitment is a key for Lin, and it can also be one for others who pursue different careers. [20]

2 LISTENING SECTION

Listen to a lecture on the topic you just read about.

3 QUESTION (SUMMARY)

Summarize the points made in the lecture, being sure to explain how the Reading Section deepens the understanding of the lecture passage (100 to 125 words). You have 20 minutes to plan and write your response.

4 LECTURE TRANSCRIPT

Born in Torrance, California in 1988, Jeremy Lin is an American of Chinese-Taiwanese descent. In 2012, he led the New York Knicks basketball team to victory. For that year, he was the most talked about NBA player. His performance led to the phenomenon known as "Linsanity." At 1.91 meters, he is one of the few Asians in the NBA. He has been traded to many teams since his days with the Knicks.

Lin attended Harvard University, and he distinguished himself in his academic studies. He also played on the basketball team. He endured racial discrimination at that time. During the games, some people shouted insults, calling him "Wonton Soup" and "Sweet and Sour Pork." He is known for his calm and kind nature. His ability to remain composed in the presence of meanness is attributable to his Christian family background. In several different publications, he has cited various Bible passages as his favorite. For the *Christian Post* magazine, in 2016, he said that his favorite Bible verse was Proverbs 16:3: "Commit to the Lord whatever you do, and your plans will succeed." In the eyes of many people, Jeremy Lin is a success and role model.

5 BIBLE FOR GLOBAL LITERACY

"Commit to the Lord whatever you do, and he will establish your plans." (Proverbs 16:3 [NIV])

「あなたの業を主にゆだねれば，計らうことは固く立つ。」（箴言 16 章 3 節）

　聖書は「旧約聖書」（ヘブライ語聖書）と「新約聖書」に分けられます。（注：カトリックでは，これらに加えて「旧約聖書続編」を聖書の一部である第二正典としています。）「旧約聖書」には，神による世界の創造の物語やイスラエル民族の歴史，古代イスラエル文学等が含まれます。上記の言葉は旧約聖書中の一書である『箴言』から取られています。

　『箴言』は，古代イスラエル文学，細かく言えば"知恵文学"というジャンルに属します。知恵文学とは，一言で言えば人生の深い意味を様々な文学形式や文体で追求したものです。旧約聖書の知恵文学には格言，詩，物語等が含まれ，比喩，擬人法，皮肉といった様々な修辞技法が用いられています。その教えは年少者への教育をはじめ，年配者が人生を振り返る際にも示唆を与えるものと言えます。「箴言」というタイトルは，漢訳聖書が元になっています。「格言集」と言い換えれば分かり易いでしょうか。実際，英語のタイトルは Book of Proverbs（格言・教訓・ことわざの書）となっています。

　「果報は寝て待て」ということわざが必ずしも文字通り「寝る」ことを意味しないように，聖書の「箴言」も比喩・格言として解釈することが大切です。ジェレミー・リンも，この言葉を掲げれば全ての計画はいつもうまくいくと信じているわけではないでしょう。この言葉が説いているのは，謙虚であること，つまり自分よりも大きな存在である神に身を委ねる姿勢を持つことの大切さなのです。

6 CULTURAL NOTES

　北米には，Big Four と呼ばれる団体競技のプロスポーツの組織があります。フットボール（NFL），野球（MLB），バスケットボール（NBA），アイスホッケー（NHL）です。その構成員は「地元の」チームです。人々は，基本的には自分の出身地のチームの試合を観戦して応援します。実際の観戦チケットが手に入らなければ，家族や友人とテレビで観戦するか，街の「スポーツ・バー」で観戦します。スポーツ観戦は，アメリカの日常的な娯楽です。ジェレミー・リンが所属したニックス（ニューヨーク）は特に人気が高く，「コートサイドチケット」と呼ばれる，コートのすぐ近くの座席のチケットは高値が付き，企業が年間チケットを購入して接待に使う例もあるほどです。

　ところで，アメリカでのスポーツには「シーズン」があります。春夏がフットボールのシーズンであるのに対し，秋冬はバスケットボールのシーズンです。これは，バスケットボールが屋内スポーツであることが理由ですが，そのため，学生時代に春夏はフットボールを，秋冬はバスケットボールをしていたという選手もいます。

7 READING SECTION NOTES

l. 5.　spectacular　壮観な

l. 6.　insanely　とてつもなく（賞賛の意味を込めて）

l. 9.　commit　〜にすべてをささげる

l.14.　humble　謙虚な

l.14.　brag　自慢する

l.18.　humility　謙遜

8 LECTURE NOTES

l. 2.　descent　子孫

l. 7.　distinguish oneself in　〜の分野で目覚しい功績を立てる

l. 8.　endure　耐える

l. 8.　racial discrimination　人種差別

l.12.　attribute to　〜のおかげと考える

9 SUMMARY SAMPLE

Jeremy Lin, one of the few Asian American basketball players in the NBA, was born in California. He has played for many different teams. According to the Reading Section, he scored 38 points for the New York Knicks in one game against their rivals, the Los Angeles Lakers in 2012. Fans were so happy, that they made up a special word for his talent: "Linsanity."

While attending Harvard University, Lin played on the basketball team, but he experienced discrimination. He was calm when people called him names such as "Wonton Soup," during his college games. His Christianity has taught him to be composed. His success in basketball is mentioned in both the Reading Section and the Lecture, but the latter states that he also did well in his Harvard studies. His talent, his kindness, and his success make him a role model.

10 CHRISTIANITY AROUND YOU

<Temperance 節制>

Temperance is a virtue encouraged by the Bible. It refers to maintaining self-control in many different areas of life. Jeremy Lin showed temperance in his reaction to the people who insulted him and called him "Wonton Soup." He remained calm and gentle despite the prejudice at the basketball games. Temperance also refers to avoiding addictions, such as alcoholism and drug abuse. The Temperance Movement warns people about the dangers of alcohol and drug abuse. The ideal is self-control whether in regard to human interactions or to eating, drinking, or consuming addictive substances.

Chapter 6 / *Manny Pacquiao*

1 READING SECTION

Read the following passage for 3 minutes.

Manny Pacquiao is a successful professional boxer in the Philippines. On January 16, 2019, Pacquiao gave a press conference standing beside his challenger for the welterweight (140-147 lb) boxing title match that was to be held at the MGM Grand Hotel and Casino in Las Vegas. In his pre-fight manner, Pacquiao spoke calmly and kindly to his rival. Pacquiao concluded his comments with a quotation from the Bible:

> Let not the wise man glory in his wisdom,
> Let not the mighty man glory in his might,
> Nor let the rich man glory in his riches ....

The quotation is taken from Jeremiah 9:23 in the Bible. It tells about the importance of humility. Human beings should not brag about their talents. Great scholars should not show off their intelligence. Rich people should not boast about their property, and strong men should not make other people miserable by emphasizing their power.

Although Pacquiao can be fierce in the ring, he usually speaks in a quiet voice at press conferences. He demonstrates the qualities mentioned in the quoted Bible words. And, oh, by the way: he won the Las Vegas fight three days later!

2 LISTENING SECTION

Listen to a lecture on the topic you just read about.

3 QUESTION (SUMMARY)

Summarize the points made in the lecture, being sure to explain how the Reading Section deepens the understanding of the lecture passage (100 to 125 words). You have 20 minutes to plan and write your response.

4 LECTURE TRANSCRIPT

Born in 1978, Manny Pacquiao escaped the poverty of his life in the Philippines through education and sports. Although he dropped out of high school, he eventually passed the high school equivalency examination in 2007. It was boxing that was to be his major springboard into fame and money. He is a champion in several weight classes, including flyweight, lightweight, and welterweight. In the 2000s, he was named "Fighter of the Decade." According to *Forbes* magazine, he was the second highest paid athlete in the world as of 2015.

Besides boxing, Pacquiao is involved in many other activities in the Philippines. He is a major television personality. He has done some acting and has recorded songs. He has also entered the world of politics in the country. In 2010, he was elected to the House of Representatives. In 2016, he began a six-year term as a senator. Even though he was once a high school dropout, he was awarded an honorary doctorate at Southwestern University in Cebu. After receiving the honorary award, he enrolled in actual college courses. Presently, he is a Colonel in the Reserve Forces of the Philippine Army. He is certainly a multi-talented man.

"... Do not let the wise boast in their wisdom, do not let the mighty boast in their might, do not let the wealthy boast in their wealth." (Jeremiah 9:23 [NRSV])

「… 知恵ある者は，その知恵を誇るな。力ある者は，その力を誇るな。富ある者は，その富を誇るな。」（エレミヤ書 9 章 23 節）

　この言葉は，旧約聖書に登場する預言者エレミヤが，神からの伝言（託宣）として人々に語った言葉からの引用です。聖書に登場する「預言者」とは「神から言葉を預かって，その言葉を他の人々に伝える人」を意味します。したがって，未来の出来事を言い当てるとされる「予言者」とは意味合いが異なります。エレミヤはそうした預言者の一人であり，「エレミヤ書」は預言者エレミヤの生涯や，エレミヤが伝えた神の言葉を記した書です。

　預言者の言葉には，高慢な人間に対する戒めや叱責の言葉，そして落胆している人々への慰めと励ましの言葉の両方が含まれます。上記の言葉は，前者の代表例と言えるでしょう。ここでは，知恵・力・富を持つこと自体は否定されていません。自分一人の力でそうしたものを得たと考えて高慢になることが戒められているのです。ここで求められているのは，知恵・力・富といったものが天から与えられたものであると認め，謙虚に生きる姿勢です。

　こうした姿勢は，ボクシングだけでなく，他のスポーツ選手にも見られます。例えば，キリスト教徒のサッカー選手が見事なシュートで得点を挙げたあと，グランドを駆け巡りながら天を指さし，上を見上げて神に感謝を捧げているシーンを目にしたことはないでしょうか。それもまた，自らの成功を誇らずに，その成功が与えられたことを神に感謝するという謙虚な姿勢の表明なのかもしれません。

6 CULTURAL NOTES

　ボクシングは，拳にグローブを着用し，パンチのみを使って相手の上半身前面と側面のみを攻撃対象とする格闘スポーツです。近代のボクシングは，16世紀にイギリスで生まれました。プロボクシングの男子の階級は，体重（ポンド／lb）により17階級に分けられます。パッキオが闘いチャンピオンとなった flyweight（フライ級）の fly はハエ，lightweight（ライト級）の light は光，welterweight（ウエルター級）の welter は強打者を意味します。そのほかにも，フェザー（羽毛）級，バンダム（小型ニワトリ）級など，階級ごとに名称がつけられています。他の格闘技でも体重による階級の区別がありますが，ボクシングでは3〜4ポンド（2〜3キロ）毎に，特に細かく分けられています。体重の数キロの差がパンチには何倍にもなって反映されるため，この階級を守ることが，選手の命を守るためには必要なのです。

7 READING SECTION NOTES

l. 2.　press conference　記者会見

l.12.　brag about　〜を自慢する

l.14.　boast about　〜を自慢する

l.15.　miserable　惨めな

l.16.　fierce　どう猛な

8 LECTURE NOTES

l. 3.　high school equivalency examination　大検

l. 4.　springboard　（〜への）出発点

l. 5.　flyweight　フライ級, lightweight　ライト級, welterweight　ウエルター級

l.10.　television personality　テレビ出演者

l.12.　House of Representatives　（二院制議会の）下院　cf.（日）衆議院

l.13.　senator　上院議員

l.14.　honorary doctorate　名誉博士号

l.16.　Colonel　大佐

Manny Pacquiao is a champion boxer. He has competed in many weight divisions. He is a confident man. According to the Reading Section, he is relaxed in the pre-fight press conferences. Pacquiao speaks kindly to his opponent. When he was young, he was poor, and he did not get a good education. Boxing changed his life. He became one of the highest paid boxers. He has been expanding his interests: Pacquiao has received an honorary doctorate. He is a famous television personality in the Philippines, and he has been elected to government offices. He is also an officer in the Philippine Reserve Army. His life is very different from his poor childhood.

10 CHRISTIANITY AROUND YOU

<Boxing and Running as New Testament Metaphors for Christian Life キリスト教的人生のたとえとしての拳闘と競争（新約聖書中の隠喩）>

Paul, the major writer of the New Testament, refers to boxing and running as metaphors for the Christian life. Just as athletes must train and work hard to achieve "the crown of victory," so too must Christians train themselves spiritually. Paul compares sports training with spiritual training. He means that practicing prayer and virtue enhances faith. Manny Pacquiao was able to springboard himself out of great poverty and deprivation of education. His victories in boxing enabled him to earn money and to pursue an education. After receiving an honorary doctorate, he was encouraged to actually enroll in college classes. Usain Bolt, the runner who performed so well in the Olympics, also achieved the highest honors in his field. Interestingly, both Bolt and Pacquiao speak about their faith and their sport. Paul may have been referring to the ancient Olympic Games when he said, "only one receives the prize in the games." In speaking about his spiritual life, he says that he "runs" and "fights" with a purpose: pleasing God (I Corinthians 9:24–27).

Chapter 7 / *Truett S. Cathy*

1 READING SECTION

Read the following passage for 3 minutes.

Truett S. Cathy created a financial empire with his fast food chain, Chick-fil-A. He was one of the most successful businessmen in America. Cathy said that his favorite Bible verse was Proverbs 22:1. "A good name is more desirable than great riches; to be esteemed better than silver or gold." 5

The Bible passage emphasizes the importance of living honestly and decently. It suggests that a reputation for being a kind and responsible person is something to be cherished. Cathy had decided on that theme for his life when he was in elementary school. He became a successful businessman, but his priority was family life and community service. Among other programs, he invested 23 million dollars over 35 years in a scholarship program for his employees. Several universities gave him honorary degrees. President George W. Bush bestowed on him the Lifetime Volunteer Service award. The Ford Automobile Factory in Atlanta gave Truett the very last Ford Taurus produced in 2006. He certainly did not need a new car, but the gift was in recognition of his "good name." 10 15

2 LISTENING SECTION

Listen to a lecture on the topic you just read about.

3 QUESTION (SUMMARY)

Summarize the points made in the lecture, being sure to explain how the Reading Section deepens the understanding of the lecture passage (100 to 125 words). You have 20 minutes to plan and write your response.

4 LECTURE TRANSCRIPT

Truett S. Cathy was born in Eatonton, Georgia (US) in 1921. He made a fortune with his fast food chain, Chick-fil-A. He wrote several books, one of which is *Wealth, Is It Worth It?* Even though he made and gave away millions, Cathy was convinced that the care of children was more important than money. In an unusual business decision, he decided to close his restaurants on Sundays, giving employees time to be with their families and to go to church.

Cathy and his wife were "foster parents" for almost 30 years. That means they took care of orphaned children. Having lived in the "Bible Belt" (a region of many churches) most of his 92 years, he learned to be considerate of others. He created a scholarship for his employees—they could work part-time and go to college part-time.

Among the organizations that Cathy supported are the Boy Scouts of America and the Winshape Foundation which provides money for orphans. Although he did not go to college, many universities honored Cathy for his humanitarian work.

5 BIBLE FOR GLOBAL LITERACY

"A good name is more desirable than great riches; to be esteemed is better than silver or gold." (Proverbs 22:1 [NIV])

「名誉は多くの富よりも望ましく　品位は金銀にまさる。」（箴言 22 章 1 節）

　これも旧約聖書の『箴言』に含まれる格言の一つです（『箴言』については，5 章の **BIBLE FOR GLOBAL　LITERACY** を参照）。富やお金よりも名誉や品位・品格を保つことが大切，というこの聖書の考えは武士道の精神に通じるところがあり，日本人にもわかりやすい言葉ではないでしょうか。実際，明治時代初期にキリスト教信仰を得た日本人の多くは士族（旧武士階級）の者が多かったと言われています。『武士道』を記した新渡戸稲造もそうでした。

　最近の聖書学には，箴言に限らず，聖書全体を文化人類学でいう「名誉と恥」の文化から読み直す動きがあります。従来の西洋的な聖書解釈が必ずしも正しいとは限らない，ということかもしれません。

　ちなみに，以下のイラストの石板上部に描かれているのは「イサク」（ヘブライ語）で，旧約聖書に登場するアブラハムの息子の名です（元々は「笑う・笑い」の意味）。「イサク」は，ヘブライ語の発音ではイツハークで，英語では Isaac となりアイザックと発音されます。哲学者・物理学者のアイザック・ニュートンや，バイオリニストのイツァーク・パールマンの名はここから来ています。

6 CULTURAL NOTES

　Foster parent（里親）とは，通常の親権を有さずに児童を養育する者のことです。アメリカでは年間12万組の養子縁組が行われており，死別，貧困，虐待などの理由で，実の親元で暮らすことができない要保護児童の約77％が里親や養子縁組などの制度により新たな「家庭」を得ているという報告があります。日本では，要保護児童の90％強が施設で暮らすことになっている実態と大きな違いがあります。トゥルエット・キャシー氏が暮らすジョージア州は，「バイブル・ベルト（聖書地帯）」と呼ばれる，アメリカの中西部から南東部にかけて複数の州にまたがって広がる地域にあたり，宗教的に保守的なプロテスタントの人々が多い地域です。教会への出席率の高さも特徴で，聖書の教えを実践しようとする人が多いと考えられます。

7 READING SECTION NOTES

l. 1.　empire　帝国
l. 2.　Chick–fil-A　チックフィレイ（ジョージア州カレッジパークに本社を置く鶏肉料理に特化したレストラン）
l. 7.　decently　礼儀正しく
l. 7.　reputation　高い評価
l. 8.　cherish　大事にする
l.10.　priority　優先すること
l.11.　invest　出資する
l.13.　honorary degree　名誉学位
l.14.　bestow　（名誉などを）授ける
l.17.　in recognition of　（功績を）称えて

8 LECTURE NOTES

l. 1.　make a fortune　富を築く
l. 9.　orphaned children　孤児たち
l.10.　considerate　思いやりのある
l.14.　orphan　孤児
l.16.　humanitarian　人道（主義）的な

9 SUMMARY SAMPLE

Truett S. Cathy was a very successful businessman. He created a fast food chain which earned him much money. The Lecture says that he wrote a book entitled, *Wealth, Is it Worth It?* As the title might suggest, money was not the most important thing to Cathy. He even closed his restaurant on Sundays, encouraging workers to spend time with family. According to the Reading Section he provided scholarships for his employees so that they could work part-time and study part-time. He was a generous man who was respected in his community. The Reading Section says that the Ford Company gave him a car. Cathy was so rich, he really did not need a new car. The Company just wanted to honor Cathy for being such a thoughtful businessman.

10 CHRISTIANITY AROUND YOU

<Care of Orphans 孤児の世話>

The Bible consistently exhorts Christians to "take care of orphans and widows." Many orphanages and homes for the elderly are operated by Christian workers. Truett S. Cathy contributed much of his money to supporting orphanages. The movie, *Blues Brothers*, is a funny film about two men who are determined to raise money to save their former orphanage, a Roman Catholic institution, from closing down. In recent years, there has been a movement to place children in homes with families instead of orphanages. Psychologists conclude that it is better for the child to be in a home with a mother, father, and a one or two brothers and sisters. In the smaller family unit, the child does not have to compete with the many children in the crowded institutions. Both styles of orphan care are still an important part of Christian service.

Chapter 8 / *Rich Froning*

Read the following passage for 3 minutes.

Rich Froning is a four-time winner of the CrossFit championship. He has earned the title, "The Fittest Man on Earth." He is not shy about his love of the Bible. Jeremiah 29:11 is one of his favorite Bible verses: "For I know the plans I have for you, declares the Lord, plans to prosper you and not to harm you, plans to give you hope and a future ..." 5

In his autobiography, *First: What It Takes to Win*, Froning talks about his childhood. Once, his father told him to move a large number of cement blocks to another location. When the task was completed, the father said that maybe the blocks should be put in yet another 10 place. His loving father was encouraging his son to build muscle. Of course, the effect was that Rich began developing the body that would earn him so many titles and so much prize money.

Froning seems to recognize his life's resemblance to Jeremiah 29: 11-13. Only as a successful man has Rich come to more fully appre- 15 ciate how God intends for us to "prosper." We may not see the reason for various events in our lives, but in the future we may smile at how well things have developed for us.

2 LISTENING SECTION

Listen to a lecture on the topic you just read about.   Track 08

3 QUESTION (SUMMARY)

Summarize the points made in the lecture, being sure to explain how the Reading Section deepens the understanding of the lecture passage (100 to 125 words). You have 20 minutes to plan and write your response.

4 LECTURE TRANSCRIPT

Rich Froning was born in 1987 in the state of Michigan. He was the grand champion of the CrossFit Games which have been held annually since 2007. The competition includes team and individual categories. Weightlifting and gymnastics are the main events. Additionally, there are surprise events which are announced shortly before the games begin. He has won over 1,050,000 dollars in prize money. Froning has been declared "The Fittest Man on Earth" at four different competitions, 2011, 2012, 2013 and 2014. He also competes in team events. His team, CrossFit Mayhem Freedom, won first place in 2015, 2016, and 2018. Fans are impressed with his gentle nature. He has said, "It's not necessarily that I like to win, but I hate losing more." Although he is strong, he does have some limitations: in 2010, he slipped several times in the rope climbing event.

Other athletes are surprised that Froning does not follow the usual diet and training regimen. He enjoys eating peanut butter, and he drinks whole milk. Those are usually forbidden foods in the CrossFit movement. He does strenuous exercise many times a day. Unlike others in the sport, he prefers not to take a day off from training. Obviously, his schedule works well for him.

"For I know the plans I have for you, ... plans to prosper you and not to harm you, plans to give you hope and a future." (Jeremiah 29:11 [NIV])

「わたしは，あなたたちのために立てた計画をよく心に留めている …。それは平和の計画であって，災いの計画ではない。将来と希望を与えるものである。」（エレミヤ書29章11節）

　これも，旧約聖書『エレミヤ書』の言葉です（『エレミヤ書』については，6章の **BIBLE FOR GLOBAL LITERACY** を参照）。

　『エレミヤ書』は，悲惨な出来事とそれに伴う大変な苦しみ，そしてその後に見えてくる希望について記しています。悲惨な出来事とは，ユダ王国が強大なバビロニア帝国に滅ぼされ支配されたことに他なりません。ユダ王国とは，神の民イスラエルが北と南の王国に分裂した後の，南側の王国です。ユダ王国内の指導者をはじめとする主だった人々は，母国を追われ，「補囚」としてバビロニア帝国に連行されて行きました（いわゆる「バビロン補囚」）。「補囚」は，神の民を襲った最大の災難の一つでした。預言者エレミヤは，そのような状況において，希望の言葉を「神の言葉」として民に伝えます。人間の目には絶望的な状況においても，実は「わたし＝神」は希望が持てる未来を民のために秘かに用意している。それが，苦しむ民にエレミヤが伝えた言葉でした。

　もっとも，そうした聖書の歴史的背景や前後の文脈にとらわれず，個人が感じるままに上記の言葉が引用されたり，壁飾り等の言葉として用いられたりしている場合がアメリカ合衆国では多々あります。フロニングの引用は，そのような聖書の自由な解釈の例と言えます。

6 CULTURAL NOTES

　クロスフィットとは，グレッグ・グラスマンによりアメリカで 2000 年に設立されたフィットネス団体です。高い運動強度で行われるフィットネス・プログラムを推奨し，競技スポーツとして毎年，世界大会を開催しています。クロスフィットには，歩く・走る・起き上がる・拾う・持ち上げる・押す・引く・跳ぶなどの「日常生活で繰り返し行う動作」をベースに，筋力トレーニング・有酸素トレーニング・柔軟トレーニングを交互に織り交ぜた数千種類のメニューが用意されており，継続していくことで身体全体が鍛えられ，日常生活の動作が楽になるのを実感できるトレーニング方法であると言われています。アメリカで，軍や警察の育成・サバイバルトレーニングに取り入れられたのをきっかけに，多くの人々に支持されるようになりました。(https://fitness.reebok.jp/training/whatiscrossfit/)

7 READING SECTION NOTES

l. 7.　autobiography　自叙伝

l. 9.　cement block　セメントのブロック

l.13.　prize money　賞金

l.14.　resemblance　類似

l.16.　prosper　繁栄する

8 LECTURE NOTES

l.13.　athlete　運動選手

l.14.　regimen　食事療法

l.14.　whole milk　成分無調整牛乳

l.15.　forbidden　禁じられた

l.16.　strenuous exercise　激しい運動

Rich Froning is a CrossFit champion. He has been described as the "Fittest Man on Earth." The Reading Section says that when he was a boy, his father gave him chores which built up his muscles. The games have both individual and team contests. He has won in both categories. The Cross-Fit games involve weightlifting and gymnastics plus other events that are not announced in advance. In 2010, one unannounced event was rope climbing. He slipped several times. Although he is a champion, he does things differently. He eats foods which other CrossFit people avoid, and he does not take a day off from training.

10 CHRISTIANITY AROUND YOU

<Humility 謙遜>

Many years ago, Mac Davis, a country singer, sang a song that had many people laughing. *It's Hard to Be Humble* is a funny song about a man who is impressed with himself. He talks about being so popular and good look-ing. Mac Davis was actually making fun of people who are vain. His song is a lesson in how not to behave. The song was a hit at parties; people sang it out loud. Of course, everybody understood that the senti-ments of the song were the exact opposite of the way mature people should behave and think. The song was popular because the ideas were so ridicu-lous:

Oh Lord, it's hard to be humble

When you're perfect in every way,

I can't look in the mirror

Cause I get better looking each day.

Rich Froning, the CrossFit champion, campaigns against that kind of arrogance. His physique is enviable. And his physical strength is amazing. Yet he always cites Galatians 6:14 which says "May I never boast except in the Cross of Christ Jesus ..." The world loves beautiful and successful people, and sometimes less-attractive and less-talented people are intimidated. It is encouraging to note the humility of people like Rich Froning.

Chapter 9 / *Rikako Ikee*

1 READING SECTION

Read the following passage for 3 minutes.

Japanese swimming champion, Rikako Ikee, won many medals at the 2018 Asian Games held in Singapore. She is the first woman selected as the Most Valuable Player at the Games. In February 2019, she was diagnosed with leukemia. Since her illness, Ikee has tweeted several messages which seem to be attempts at cheering up her fans! One of the messages is a paraphrase of the famous Bible quotation, I Corinthians 10:13. In her rewording, Ikee said, "God will not give me any trials that I am unable to overcome." The idea is that God is aware of our challenges and will give us strength to cope with the difficulty. The actual words are: "He (God) will not let you be tempted beyond what you can bear."

When faced with hard times, many people are tempted to give up. Other people develop positive attitudes. Not only does the latter group hope to survive the problem, they believe that something good might happen! Ikee occasionally leaves the hospital and does fun things like going to Disneyland, or cheering on her swim teammates at Nihon University. When she learned that many people are volunteering to donate bone marrow (necessary in leukemia treatment), Ikee was very happy. Her concern for her fans, and her response to the spike in bone marrow volunteers gives insight into her character: she is loved and she is loving.

2 LISTENING SECTION

Listen to a lecture on the topic you just read about.

3 QUESTION (SUMMARY)

Summarize the points made in the lecture, being sure to explain how the Reading Section deepens the understanding of the lecture passage (125 to 175 words). You have 20 minutes to plan and write your response.

4 LECTURE TRANSCRIPT

Rikako Ikee is a champion swimmer. She was born on July 4, 2000 and is currently a student at Nihon University. She is an international star athlete who has won numerous awards and prizes. Notably, she received six gold and two silver medals at the 2018 Asian Games in Indonesia. Her outstanding performances are in the 50, 100, and 200 meter races, and in the butterfly competition. After returning to Japan, Ikee was notified that she was selected as the Most Valuable Player for those games. She is the first female to be so honored. Because of this historic first, Ikee decided to return to Indonesia to collect her prizes and to acknowledge the importance of the event.

In February 2019, Ikee was diagnosed with leukemia. She requires alternating outpatient and inpatient treatments at the hospital. During her times away from the hospital, she has appeared at a swim meet, cheering on her university team. She has even been photographed smiling during a Disneyland visit. A well-loved athlete, she has received heartfelt greetings from fellow international competitors. One indication of the respect people have for her is the spike in phone calls and visits to medical centers; fans want to know how they can volunteer to donate bone marrow. When she heard about the overwhelming response of bone marrow donors, Ikee said that she was happy about the increase in leukemia awareness.

"No temptation has overtaken you except what is common to mankind. And God is faithful; he will not let you be tempted beyond what you can bear. But when you are tempted, he will also provide a way out so that you can endure it." (I Corinthians 10:13 [NIV])

「あなたがたを襲った試練で，人間として耐えられないようなものはなかったはずです。神は真実な方です。あなたがたを耐えられないような試練に遭わせることはなさらず，試練と共に，それに耐えられるよう，逃れる道をも備えていてくださいます。」（コリントの信徒への手紙一 10 章 13 節）

　聖書の言葉は，その言葉が記されている前後の文脈や時代背景，そして聖書全体の思想に沿って意味を解釈することが原則と言えます。しかし，前章の **BIBLE FOR GLOBAL LITERACY** に記したように，時にはそのような原則から離れて特定の言葉のみが注目されている場合もあります。実際，聖書の言葉を引用してきた古今東西の人々の多くは歴史学者や聖書学者ではありませんでした。それらの人々は，人生の様々な歩みの中で出会った聖書の言葉を自分の心の支えとしてきたのです。

　ここに登場する『コリントの信徒への手紙一』10 章 13 節のテーマは試練・苦しみです。どんな試練であっても必ず耐えられると説くこの言葉は，前後の文脈にとらわれずに多くの人が引用してきた聖書の言葉の典型的な例と言えるでしょう。ちなみに，ここに記されている「逃れる道」とは，「逃避」の道ではなく，「脱出の道」，「乗り越える道」と言い換えられるものです。

　池江璃花子さんは，突然襲ってきた試練の中で「神様は乗り越えられない試練は与えない」とツイッターに記しました。池江さんの言葉は，一字一句聖書の言葉そのままというわけではないかもしれませんが，十分に聖書の精神と合致した言葉であると言えるでしょう。

6 CULTURAL NOTES

　池江選手が診断された急性リンパ性白血病（ALL: Acute Lymphocytic Leukemia）は，白血球の一種であるリンパ球が幼若な段階で悪性化し，がん化した細胞（白血病細胞）が無制限に増殖することで発症する病気です（https://ganjoho.jp/public/cancer/ALL/index.html）。現在，白血病治療の治療は目覚ましい進歩を遂げており，治癒して復帰したスポーツ選手も存在します。骨髄移植が治療法の一つですが，型の合うドナーの骨髄でなければ移植できません。そのため，少しでも多くの人の骨髄バンクへのドナー登録が必要不可欠なのです。

7 READING SECTION NOTES

l. 4.　diagnose　診断する

l. 4.　leukemia　白血病

l. 5.　cheer up　元気づける

l. 6.　paraphrase　言い換え

l. 7.　reword　言い換える

l.11.　tempt　〜の気にさせる

l.18.　bone marrow　骨髄

8 LECTURE NOTES

l. 4.　outstanding　傑出した

l.11.　alternating　交互の

l.13.　swim meet　水泳大会

l.15.　heartfelt　心からの

l.15.　greeting　（人を温かく）出迎えること

l.17.　spike　急増

l.19.　overwhelming　圧倒的な数の

l.19.　donor　ドナー

l.20.　awareness　認知度

In 2018, Rikako Ikee, Japanese swimming champion, received good news. She was selected as the Most Valuable Player at the Asian Games in Indonesia. In February 2019, she received bad news. She was diagnosed with leukemia. According to the Reading Section there are two kinds of people: those who get depressed when they have difficulties and those who remain hopeful. Ikee is the latter kind of person. The Lecture says that since her diagnosis, she has attended a swim meet at her school, Nihon University. Further, she has even been seen smiling at Disneyland. Clearly, Ikee thinks positively. In fact, according to the Reading Section, she sends out messages attempting to cheer her fans up. She thinks about other people. The Reading Section says that because of her, there has been a rise in the number of volunteers to donate bone marrow, which is necessary for treating leukemia.

10 CHRISTIANITY AROUND YOU

<Meditating on the Positive 物事を前向きにとらえる>

Despite her ordeal, Rikako Ikee is positive. She focuses on whatever is good, beautiful, and noble. Positive thinking has helped many people overcome difficult circumstances. The famous book, *The Power of Positive Thinking*, by Dr. Norman Vincent Peale has been shared by many people. There are many stories of people who have found relief through focus on a happy thought or a pleasing object. Nelson Mandela, the first black South African President, was imprisoned for many years. He continually read a particular poem, *Invictus*. Positive thinking is not exclusive to Christians. Other religions teach the concept as well.

1 READING SECTION

Read the following passage for 3 minutes.

Mariah Carey has been one of the top American singers since the 1990s. Eighteen of her songs have been number one in the United States, and she has received numerous music awards, including Grammy Awards, Billboard Music Awards, and MTV Video Music Awards. [5]

The concluding song on Mariah Carey's 2008 album is a ballad, *I Wish You Well*. It is about a broken romance. Carey references an abusive lover. Although the song speaks of having been "cursed" and "bruised" in the past, the woman of the ballad escapes the unhappiness. She is able to forgive the former lover. [10]

The song's lyrics include the following words: "Let him without sin cast the first stone." This is a quotation from the Bible. The line comes from a famous story in which townsmen force a "sinful" woman into Jesus' presence. They want him to apply the ancient punishment of stoning to her. She had been caught in adultery with [15] a man.

Speaking to the bloodthirsty men, Jesus uttered the famous words, "Let him who is without sin cast the first stone." In other words, Jesus was saying that only a completely innocent person could throw the first stone at her. After hearing Jesus' words, the men walked away, [20] one by one. They abandoned their plans for a public execution. It is a story about mercy. It is a reminder of the need to be forgiving and compassionate. In modern English conversation those words mean nobody is perfect, everyone makes mistakes. So, we should be cautious about condemning others.

2 LISTENING SECTION

Listen to a lecture on the topic you just read about.

3 QUESTION (SUMMARY)

Summarize the points made in the lecture, being sure to explain how the Reading Section deepens the understanding of the lecture passage (125 to 175 words). You have 20 minutes to plan and write your response.

4 LECTURE TRANSCRIPT

Mariah Carey was born in New York City. There is some confusion about the year of her birth, either 1969 or 1970. By the 1990s, she was celebrated as the *Songbird Supreme* by the Guinness World Records. Her first five songs were all on the Billboard Top 100. At various times, she has been highly praised and highly criticized. Carey's full use of her five-octave range is controversial. Some people complain that she is "showing off" when she suddenly sings and holds very high notes. Other people are amazed at that technique and insist that she is an incomparable artist. Despite the complaints of some people, Carey was named Artist of the Decade in 1999.

As with many writers, actors, and singers, Carey has used some elements of her own life in her art. As a bi-racial child, she was rejected by some relatives. She experienced a nervous breakdown, divorces, and failures in her life.

Carey's strength is manifested not only in her musical talents but also in her ability to respond positively to her critics. Her film *Glitter* was rejected by critics. During her New Year's Eve performance, it was discovered that she wasn't really singing; she was lip synching. At times, enemies laughed at her. However, like the character in her song *I Wish You Well,* she found peace and had later triumphs. Mariah, too, is able to forgive the people who had rejoiced in her failures. She is able to pray for them and to wish them well.

5 BIBLE FOR GLOBAL LITERACY

"When they kept on questioning him, he straightened up and said to them, 'Let anyone among you who is without sin be the first to throw a stone at her.'" (John 8:7 [NRSV])

「しかし，彼らがしつこく問い続けるので，イエスは身を起こして言われた。『あなたたちの中で罪を犯したことのない者が，まず，この女に石を投げなさい。』」（ヨハネによる福音書8章7節）

　これは，イエス・キリストの生涯の中でも良く知られたエピソードの中の一節です。この話でイエスは，不倫（聖書の言葉で「姦通・姦淫」）の現場で捕まった一人の女性と，その女性を石打の刑に処すべきかどうかを問いただしてきた「律法学者」や「ファリサイ派」といった人々（男性）の集団を前にします。旧約聖書の律法は，不倫した者は石打による死刑と定めていたからです。律法の厳格な遵守を主張していたこれらの人々は，愛や赦しを説くイエスがこの女性にどう対処するかを試そうとしていたようです。

　「自分に罪のない者がまず最初の石を投げよ」というイエスの返答は，そんな彼らを当惑させたことでしょう。結局，この女性に石を投げる者はありませんでした。イエスはこの言葉により，正義を振りかざして他者を断罪しようとする男性集団の高慢な姿勢を問題にしているのです。

　「人の振り見て我が振り直せ」と言いますが，実際には自分のことを棚に上げて他者を叱責することが多いのは昔も今も変わらないでしょう。現代であれば，SNS上で特定の人の言葉や行動への非難が殺到して「炎上」状態となることがあります。もちろん，差別や虐待など問題をはっきりと指摘すべきときもあります。そうではないときに，他者への安易な誹謗中傷を戒める言葉としてこの言葉を覚えておくと良いのではないでしょうか。

　ちなみに，マライア・キャリーの歌 *I Wish You Well* の歌詞には，この他にも聖書の言葉が度々登場します。どんな言葉があるのか探してみましょう。

6 CULTURAL NOTES

　マライア・キャリーは，父親はアフリカ系ベネズエラ人とアフリカ系アメリカ人の混血，母親はアイルランド系アメリカ人です。このように 2 つ以上の人種を親に持つ人は英語では "mixed race" と言います。人種の多様性（diversity）は現代アメリカの特徴です。最近では，2018 年にイギリスのハリー王子と結婚したアメリカ人女優のメーガン・マークルが，"I voice my pride in being a strong, confident mixed-race woman." と言っています。

　歌手としても女優としても成功したマライア・キャリーは，貧しかった子ども時代を忘れることはなく，1994 年から毎年夏に「キャンプ・マライア」を開催して経済的に恵まれない子供たちにプログラムを提供しています。12 〜 14 歳の子供たちが自然の中で過ごしながら，映画や写真，ファッション，料理など各自が興味のある分野を探求できるプログラムだそうです。このようなチャリティ活動を行っているのも，彼女のキリスト教的精神の現れと考えることができます。

　アメリカの夏休みは 2 〜 3 か月と長く，サマーキャンプと呼ばれるプログラムに参加することが慣習となっています。日本ではキャンプと言うと野外活動・キャンプファイヤーを想像しますが，アメリカのサマーキャンプは野外活動に止まらず，スポーツ，音楽，理系の学問系プログラムなど多岐に渡り，参加費用も期間も様々です。

7 READING SECTION NOTES

l. 8.　abusive　虐待する

l. 8.　curse　悪態をつく

l. 9.　bruise　（人の感情を）傷つける

l.13.　townsman　同じ町に住む人

l.15.　adultery　不貞（の行為）

l.17.　bloodthirsty　残虐な

l.21.　execution　処刑

l.23.　compassionate　あわれみ深い

8 LECTURE NOTES

l. 5.　octave　オクターブ

l. 7.　note　音

l. 8.　incomparable　比類のない

l.12.　bi-racial　（特に白人と黒人の）二人種の

l.13.　breakdown　衰弱

l.15.　manifest　明白に示す

l.18.　lip synching　口パク

l.20.　triumph　勝利の喜び

l.21.　rejoice　喜ぶ

9 SUMMARY SAMPLE

The American singer, Mariah Carey, is controversial. She has been called the *Songbird Supreme* by the Guinness World Records, but some people complain that she "shows off." She has a five-octave range which allows her to hold very high notes. Some people praise her technique, others criticize her. She is accustomed to complaints. As a bi-racial child, she was rejected by some relatives. People have gossiped about her failures. Her movie, *Glitter* was attacked by critics. At her New Year's Eve performance, the audience reacted negatively when they discovered that she was "lip synching." Despite these bad moments, Carey has also had some wonderful success. Her first five songs were selected for the Billboard Top 100. According to the Reading Section she has won numerous awards. The Lecture suggests that Carey has a strong character. Her song, *I Wish You Well*, tells the story of a woman who has been abused by an unfaithful lover. Despite the unkindness she has experienced, Mariah Carey enjoys her success and prays for her enemies. She wishes them well.

Chapter 11 / *Neymar*

Read the following passage for 3 minutes.

The magazines of the world have different titles for Neymar, the football player. *TIME* magazine calls him one of the most influential people in the world. *Forbes* magazine ranks him one of the three highest paid athletes. When Neymar signed a contract with the Paris-St. Germain team in 2017, many sources declared him the most expensive player. He is a controversial figure. Many people are impressed with his skill; they cite such accomplishments as his two scores in the match between Brazil and Honduras in the 2016 Summer Olympics. Other people talk about the tattoos all over his body and his "fake injuries" on the field. Recently, he wore a T-shirt with Bible words from Isaiah 54:17. "No weapon forged against you will prevail."

Neymar made a short video of himself wearing the shirt. The words seem to suggest that Neymar thinks he is at war with somebody. The Bible verse simply means that good people will be victorious over their enemies. The question is, "Who are Neymar's enemies?" Is he referring to the teams he plays against? Is he referring to a particular game referee? Although the enemy referenced on the T-shirt is a mystery, many people are completely charmed by Neymar. Fans focus on his athletic ability, his charity matches, and his love of Brazilian music. Nobody pleases everybody. Neymar seems convinced of God's protection.

2 LISTENING SECTION

Listen to a lecture on the topic you just read about.

3 QUESTION (SUMMARY)

Summarize the points made in the lecture, being sure to explain how the Reading Section deepens the understanding of the lecture passage (125 to 175 words). You have 20 minutes to plan and write your response.

4 LECTURE TRANSCRIPT

His full name is Neymar da Silva Santos Junior, but he is known the world over simply as "Neymar." He was born in Sao Paulo in 1992, and he is literally one of the most colorful players: he changes his hairstyle and color often. He has played for Paris Saint-Germain and Barcelona teams. Of course, he has played for Brazil's national team. He is one of the highest paid players in the world. He can be very dramatic on the field. At the 2018 Russia World Cup, Neymar was key to the victory over Mexico. However, his dramatic collapse and complaint of being kicked in the head was a much-discussed occurrence. After lying on the field and crying, he seemed to make a miraculous recovery. The Brazilian newspaper, *O Globo* said, "Neymar has charmed Brazil, but annoyed the whole world."

He is undoubtedly a great player, but somehow Neymar has become known for his tears. There are photos of him crying "tears of joy" after Brazil beat Costa Rica in 2018. There are "bitter tears" after his Barcelona team was beaten by Juventus. Of course, critics make fun of these pictures. Despite the emotionalism, he is a valuable high scorer. *SportsPro* magazine named him as the most marketable athlete in the world in 2012−2013. If Neymar is featured in the match, the stadium attendance is guaranteed to be large.

5 BIBLE FOR GLOBAL LITERACY

"No weapon forged against you will prevail ..." (Isaiah 54:17 [NIV])

「どのような武器があなたに対して作られても　何一つ役に立つことはない。...」（イザヤ書 54 章 17 節）

　旧約聖書の預言書『イザヤ書』には，苦しみのただ中にある人々を慰め，希望を与える言葉が，とりわけ後半部分に多く記されています（『イザヤ書』については 4 章の **BIBLE FOR GLOBAL LITERACY** 参照）。上記の言葉も，そのような慰めのメッセージの一部なのです。

　この『イザヤ書』54 章 17 節にある「武器」とは，人を責めるものという意味合いがあります。戦争だけでなく，いじめや虐待など，人を責めて窮地に追い込むものは多々あるでしょう。ネイマールも，有名人であるからこそ注目され，他者から責められることが少なくないのかもしれません。いわれなき理由で責められ苦しんでいる人にとっては，そのような状況から立ち直る力（レジリエンス）も重要になってきます。ネイマールは，そのような力につながるヒントを聖書の言葉から得たのかもしれません。

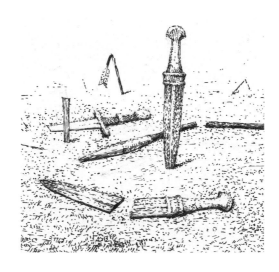

6 CULTURAL NOTES

　ネイマールはブラジル出身のサッカー選手で，ブラジル代表には 18 歳でデビューし，ペレ，ロナウドに次ぐ第 3 位の得点記録保持者です。2016 年のリオオリンピックでは，金メダルを獲っています。サントス，バルセロナといった有名なチームを経て，2017 年には史上最高額の 2 億 2200 万ユーロ相当（約 284 億円）でパリ・サンジェルマンに移籍しました。2019 年には，フォーブス誌は，メッシ，ロナウドに次いで世界で 3 番目に高収入のスポーツ選手であると報じました。

ブラジルには，どんな田舎へ行っても，カトリック教会とサッカーグランドはあると言われます。世界的な名選手を輩出する背景には，幼少期から日常的にサッカーに親しみ，格闘技とダンスをミックスしたようなカポエイラというスポーツや，ブラジル土着の踊りであるサンバを踊る上体の動きの影響を受けた独特なリズムを持った動きを自然と身につけているからなのでしょう。サッカーはまさに国民的スポーツで，ワールドカップ開催中は，人々は代表チームのプレーを見るために仕事を休んだり，雇用主が従業員が観戦できる場所を設定したりすることさえあるといいます。ブラジル代表チームは，これまでワールドカップで5回優勝しています。

7 READING SECTION NOTES

l. 6.   controversial   議論の的になる

l. 6.   figure   人物

l. 7.   accomplishment   偉業

l.10.   fake   偽の

l.15.   victorious   勝利を得た

8 LECTURE NOTES

l. 3.   literally   文字通りに

l. 8.   collapse   倒れ込み

l.10.   miraculous   奇跡的な

l.16.   emotionalism   感情過多

l.18.   featured   呼び物にする

9 SUMMARY SAMPLE

Neymar is a controversial football player. Although he plays well, he is emotional. Many people make fun of his tears. There are many photos of him crying. He has wept when his team has won. He has wept when his team has lost. He is a financial success. The Reading Section says that *Forbes* magazine ranks him as one of the highest paid athletes in the world. Neymar's personality is interesting. The Lecture states that Neymar is colorful, referring to his many changes in hairstyle and hair color. The Reading Section also says that there are so many tattoos all over his body. He is aware of the people's reactions to him. The newspaper in his own country said, "Neymar has charmed Brazil, but has annoyed the whole world." In the Reading Section Neymar describes himself as religious. He believes that God protects him.

10 CHRISTIANITY AROUND YOU

<Rosary ロザリオ>

Neymar is a man of great athletic skill. He is a man possessed of a colorful personality. Despite several publicized misdeeds, he also expresses his Christian faith. Most sources say that he is a Pentecostal Christian (their worship services are sometimes emotional); at least one source says that he is a Roman Catholic. There are many photos of him participating in the Paris Fashion week over the years. He models clothes by Jacques Balmain and other designers. Often, he wears a rosary around his neck. His rosary accessory is in keeping with his many religious tattoos.

The rosary is a collection of prayer beads which are used in devotion to Mary, the Mother of Jesus Christ. The tradition dates to the third or fourth century. It is mostly associated with the Roman Catholic Church. However, similar groups such as the Anglican and the Lutheran churches also have rosaries. Rosaries range from inexpensive to expensive. They can be made of plastic, wood, or semi-precious stones. For average Christians, rosaries are not worn. They are often hidden in the pockets of the people who pray while doing ordinary life activities. Certain nuns and priests wear large rosaries suspended from their waist belts.

1 READING SECTION

Read the following passage for 3 minutes.

As author of the famous *Harry Potter* series, J. K. Rowling has made a fortune. She has often mentioned how her life has changed. Once dependent on government welfare, she is now one of the greatest contributors to charities. She has tweeted a famous Bible verse to urge government leaders to welcome immigrants. She thinks rich countries should welcome people who are escaping poverty and persecution in their home countries. Having gained fame and money through her writings, Rowling is eager to help others. She cited the following words from the Bible: "What good will it be for a man if he gains the whole world, yet forfeits his soul?"

There are some people who rise from a life of hardship to achieve a life of comfort and ease. Unfortunately, some people become selfish after they have escaped misery. Rowling does not want to be such a person. She remembers her prior life, and she wants to extend kindness and assistance to other people who need improvement in their living conditions. Matthew 16: 26 which she quotes above is a reminder that it is meaningless to become a politically or financially powerful person if we neglect to help others. She recognizes that although she is rich and important, her real wealth comes from sharing with others. She says: "Personal happiness lies in knowing that life is not a checklist of acquisition or achievement. Your qualifications are not your life."

2 LISTENING SECTION

Listen to a lecture on the topic you just read about.

3 QUESTION (SUMMARY)

Summarize the points made in the lecture, being sure to explain how the Reading Section deepens the understanding of the lecture passage (125 to 175 words). You have 20 minutes to plan and write your response.

4 LECTURE TRANSCRIPT

J. K. Rowling is a name revered all over the world. She was born in Gloucestershire, England on July 31, 1965. Of course, creating the *Harry Potter* series is the work for which she is most famous. Her life has been a roller-coaster ride of good and bad moments. Her early home life was not perfect; her mother was very sick, and her father had a difficult personality. She went on to graduate from Exeter University. Her first marriage in 1995 ended in divorce. Before she became a celebrated author, she was a single mother living on government assistance. Eventually she achieved prominence as a writer. One critic expressed amazement that her books have revived children's interest in reading. Her commitment to various charities and her defense of people who suffer discrimination are equally as important to her as her success.

Creating the *Harry Potter* series has made her an extremely wealthy woman. Undoubtedly, she and her family can now afford a luxurious lifestyle. At one point, she was declared a billionaire. However, she lost that status. Having given away a huge portion of her fortune, she has been removed from the official list of billionaires. Even so, as of 2016, she was still listed as the 197th richest person in the United Kingdom. She attends church on occasion, but she acknowledges that she disagrees with some "church ideas." Rowling encourages the rich countries of the world to welcome immigrants. Clearly, she demonstrates that her priority is people, not money.

5 BIBLE FOR GLOBAL LITERACY

"What good will it be for someone to gain the whole world, yet forfeit their soul? ..."
(Matthew 16:26 [NIV])

「人は，たとえ全世界を手に入れても，自分の命を失ったら，何の得があろうか。…」（マタイによる福音書 16 章 26 節）

　上記の言葉は，イエス・キリストが弟子に語った言葉の一部です。独特の言い回しで語られているこの教えは，物や情報に満ちあふれた現代社会に生きる人々に，何が一番大切であるのかを改めて問う言葉と言えます。自分のいのちだけでなく，すべてのいのちを大切にすることは，聖書の根本的な思想の一つなのです。

　ロシアの文豪でキリスト者でもあったトルストイの民話に，『人にはどれだけの土地がいるか』があります。農夫のパホームは，一日に自分が歩いただけの土地を手に入れられると聞き，ひたすら歩き続けます。自分はもっと歩ける。もっと欲しい。あともう少しだけ…。そうしてあまりにも急いで歩き過ぎたパホームが日没を前に息絶えるという話です。

　『ハリー・ポッター』の著者として知られる J．K．ローリングは，他者に与えることの大切さを説くことで，すべてのいのちの尊さを訴えているのかもしれません。

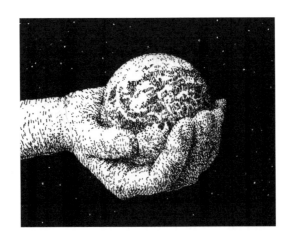

6 CULTURAL NOTES

　聖書では，裕福な人はそうでない人に施すことを推奨しています（第2章参照）。これをチャリティ（慈善）と言います。チャリティは，1980年代に音楽を媒介としてそれまでにない世界的なものに発展しました。当時，干ばつや内乱で数十万人の餓死者が出ていたエチオピアの救済のため，イギリスではU2のボノ，ディビッド・ボウイ，フィル・コリンズといったミュージシャンによって，「バンド・エイド」，「ライブ・エイド」といったチャリティコンサートが開かれました。アメリカでも，マイケル・ジャクソンやレイ・チャールズ，ライオネル・リッチーらアメリカのトップスター達が，やはりアフリカの飢餓救済のために立ち上がり，*We Are the World* という楽曲に関わる収益を寄付するチャリティが行われました。

　最近では，本章のJ.K.ローリングやビル・ゲイツ（第2章），イギリス人歌手のエルトン・ジョンやアメリカ人女優のエリザベス・テイラーなどの有名人がチャリティ活動を活発に行っています。ナタリー・ポートマン，ヒラリー・ダフ，リンジー・ローハンなど若手の「セレブ」もチャリティ活動をしています。

7 READING SECTION NOTES

l. 3.　welfare　福祉事業

l. 3.　contributor　寄付者

l. 6.　persecution　迫害

l.10.　forfeit　失う

l.11.　hardship　苦難

l.13.　misery　惨めな状態

l.21.　acquisition　獲得

8 LECTURE NOTES

l. 1.　revere　（成功した人を）尊敬する

l. 2.　Gloucestershire　グロスタシャー州（イングランド南西部）

l. 4.　roller-coaster ride　ジェットコースターに乗ること

　　　roller-coaster　（ジェットコースターのように）波瀾万丈の

l. 7.　divorce　離婚

l. 7.　celebrated　著名な

l. 8.　achieve prominence　成功を収める

l.10. revive 復活させる

l.15. billionaire 億万長者

l.16. fortune 財産

9 SUMMARY SAMPLE

J. K. Rowling is well-known for her *Harry Potter* books. Her writing has made her very wealthy. Critics claim that her books have increased children's interest in reading. But her life has not always been so happy. When she was young, her mother was sick and Rowling had problems with her father. She graduated from university and got married, but later she got divorced. Of course, her life changed greatly because of her books. According to the Lecture, Rowling lost her status as a billionaire for a good reason: she gave away much of her money to charities. She understands poverty. Once she had been a young single mother depending on government assistance. Now that she enjoys a good life, she is eager to help others. The Reading Section says that sometimes people escape misery and become very comfortable. But it disturbs Rowling that such lucky people sometimes become selfish. She does not want to be like that.

Chapter 13 / *Chadwick Boseman*

1 READING SECTION

Read the following passage for 3 minutes.

Chadwick Boseman addressed the 2018 graduates of Howard University in Washington, D.C. That university is predominantly African American. Boseman, himself, was among the distinguished alumni. He graduated in 2000. His stature as a major film actor put him in high demand as a public speaker. The students in the Howard audience were very familiar with Boseman's strong and dignified character, T'Challa, in *Black Panther*. However, his address to the students expressed great humility. He clearly stated that he owed his success in films to generations of earlier African American actors who experienced terrible discrimination. Boseman spoke about such actors being forced to portray uneducated servants. Because of the encouragement from actors before him, he could finally act in a film biography of a black supreme court justice and, of course, in the role of an African prince. He cited I Corinthians 3:6: "I planted the seed, Apollos watered it, but God has been making it grow."

In the Bible, Paul did not want to take all of the credit for his accomplishments. He indicated that he was one of a series of people who have taught Christianity and who have caused it to flourish. Paul used a farm illustration to suggest that many workers contributed to the growth of Christianity. Similarly, Boseman said that many black actors of the past were denied prominent roles in movies, but their persistence caused directors and producers to finally allow modern African Americans such as himself to star in important films. No longer limited to minor roles as servants in movies, black actors com-

2 LISTENING SECTION

Listen to a lecture on the topic you just read about.

3 QUESTION (SUMMARY)

Summarize the points made in the lecture, being sure to explain how the Reading Section deepens the understanding of the lecture passage (125 to 175 words). You have 20 minutes to plan and write your response.

4 LECTURE TRANSCRIPT

Chadwick Boseman was born in South Carolina, USA in 1976. He died in August 2020. He was a movie and television star. Originally, he acted in film biographies of famous African Americans. However, his most famous film was *Black Panther*, made in 2016. The movie is about a mythical African kingdom which has advanced technology. It was one of the biggest money-making movies of the year. Boseman continued to act in the highly popular Marvel Comics productions. Even now, his face is definitely recognizable, appearing on many movie posters. However, his original plan was to distinguish himself as a stage and film writer. He actually wrote a powerful play while in high school. He wrote the drama, *Crossroads*, about the killing of a high school student. The play was staged at his high school. He said he only got involved in acting so that he could understand how to be a better writer.

Although Boseman had fans from all over the world, he celebrated his African American culture. DNA testing has verified that he was a descendant of several different groups of African people: Yoruba people of Nigeria, and Krio and Limba people of Sierra Leone. In addition to his film career,

Boseman taught at the prestigious Schomburg Research Center in Harlem, New York. That center highlights the achievements of the great African American scholars, writers, and scientists. He was the perfect combination of entertainer and teacher of culture.

20

5 BIBLE FOR GLOBAL LITERACY

"I planted the seed, Apollos watered it, but God has been making it grow." (I Corinthians 3:6 [NIV])

「わたしは植え，アポロは水を注いだ。しかし，成長させてくださったのは神です。」（コリントの信徒への手紙一3章6節）

　『コリントの信徒への手紙一』は，使徒パウロがコリントにあった教会（信徒の集まり）に宛てて記した手紙の一つです。コリントはギリシアの都市で，新約聖書の時代には古代ローマ帝国の植民都市として栄えていました。パウロはかつてこの町に宣教師として赴き，教会を始めました。その後，この教会は発展するのですが，同時に複数の有力者が対立し，教会内で嘆かわしい派閥争いが起こっていたようです。

　上記の箇所は，「植える，水を注ぐ，成長する」という植物の隠喩（メタファー）により，コリントの教会の起源と発展の過程を描いています。この教会の基礎を築いたのは使徒パウロでしたが，後にアポロという名の別の指導者が教えたこともありました。その他にも，複数の有力者がこの教会の発展に貢献したことでしょう。しかし，ここでパウロが強調しているのは，最終的に発展全体を導いたのは，いかなる人間でもなく目には見えない神であるという視点です。その視点を通して，成長・発展・成功の理由を特定の人物の貢献のみに帰することの愚かさをパウロは伝えようとしたのでした。

　この教えは，個人の人生にも当てはまります。俳優チャドウィック・ボーズマンは，上記の聖書の言葉を引用することで，今の自分があるのは，差別と闘ってきた多くのアフリカ系アメリカ人の先輩がいたからであると言いたかったのでしょうか。聖書の言葉は，このようにして多くの人々に謙遜の大切さを教えてきました。

6 CULTURAL NOTES

　「マーベル」は，アイアンマン，スパイダーマンなどのアメリカのスーパーヒーローを生んだコミック会社です。2009 年にウォルト・ディズニー・カンパニーに買収され，近年，もとはコミック（漫画）であったヒーローが実写版で映画化されています。2018 年公開の『ブラック・パンサー』もマーベルの実写版映画で，ワカンダという国の若き国王ティ・チャラであり，ブラックパンサーというヒーローでもある主人公を，チャドウィック・ボーズマンが演じています。この映画は，監督から出演者まで大半がアフリカ系アメリカ人であることでも注目を集めました。

7 READING SECTION NOTES

- l. 2.　predominantly　圧倒的に多い
- l. 3.　alumni　卒業生（alumnus の複数形）
- l. 6.　dignified　威厳のある
- l.16.　Paul　キリスト教の使徒・聖人。キリスト教布教の偉大な功労者。
- l.16.　take credit for　自分の手柄にする
- l.21.　prominent role　大きな役割
- l.24.　command　意のままにする

8 LECTURE NOTES

- l. 4.　mythical　架空の
- l.15.　verify　実証する
- l.15.　descendant　子孫

l.16.　Yoruba　ヨルバ族（主にナイジェリア南西部に居住するアフリカの民族）

l.17.　Krio　または Creole は，シエラレオネ共和国の民族

l.17.　Limba　リンバ族（シエラレオネ共和国の中で 3 番目に多い部族）

l.17.　Sierra Leone　シエラレオネ共和国（西アフリカ）

l.18.　Schomburg Research Center　アフリカ系アメリカ人に関して優れた研究を行っている研究所

9 SUMMARY SAMPLE

Chadwick Boseman was famous for acting as the Marvel Comics hero, T'Challa, in the 2016 film, *Black Panther*. That story is about a mythological African kingdom which has advanced technology. According to the Reading Section, in the old days, blacks were most often represented in films as servants. *Black Panther* shows Boseman's dignified portrayal of a strong prince. He took pride in his African American culture. Originally, Boseman planned to be a writer. When he was in high school, he wrote a drama about a student who had been killed. The drama, *Crossroads,* was staged at his school. Later, Boseman acted in a movie about a real-life African American supreme court judge. Not only was Boseman a writer and an actor, he taught at a famous research center in Harlem, New York. The Reading Section says that Boseman gave the graduation speech at Howard University in 2018. Boseman impressed students with his fame and with his humility.

Chapter 14 / *Tomihiro Hoshino*

1 READING SECTION

Read the following passage for 3 minutes.

Tomihiro Hoshino was a strong young high school student in Gunma Prefecture when he had to carry heavy buckets of pig manure up a steep slope. He had to fertilize the fields near his house. One day, exhausted from his many trips carrying the buckets, he saw a grave marked by a cross and a verse from the Bible: "Come to me, all you who are weary and burdened, and I will give you rest" (Matthew 11:28).

He was not a Christian, and he did not understand the words, but he liked the idea of "rest." Years later, when he was 24 years old, he was completely paralyzed while teaching gymnastics to his junior high school students. He became burdened with depression. He was burdened with guilt because his mother exhausted herself in helping him. He was burdened by the loss of his physical strength.

In 1974, Hoshino became a Christian. Gradually he began to focus on the positive elements of his life: he got married, and he became a world-respected "mouth artist." He has his own museum in Azuma Village, Japan. His works have been displayed in New York and other famous cities. Now, as he studies the Bible, he understands the meaning of the words he had encountered while hauling fertilizer: God is eager to comfort us. Hoshino's art reflects his happiness. Even though he is no longer a junior high school teacher, his art exhibitions and his beautiful books are lessons in discovering peace and beauty.

2 LISTENING SECTION

Listen to a lecture on the topic you just read about.

3 QUESTION (SUMMARY)

Summarize the points made in the lecture, being sure to explain how the Reading Section deepens the understanding of the lecture passage (125 to 175 words). You have 20 minutes to plan and write your response.

4 LECTURE TRANSCRIPT

Tomihiro Hoshino was born in Gunma Prefecture in Japan in 1946. He is an accomplished poet, painter, and collaborator on choral music. He cultivated these skills after his terrible accident in the gymnasium of the junior high school where he had been a physical education teacher. In 1970, he was demonstrating a maneuver to his students when he fell during a gymnastic vaulting routine; his career as a teacher ended. He was paralyzed from the neck down. The next nine years of his life were spent in the hospital where he endured several life-threatening episodes. He attributes his survival to his mother's constant care, and to the love of a Christian woman whom he married in 1981.

He remembers an episode when his hospital roommate was being transferred to another hospital. Staff members and other patients decided to prepare a farewell card. Of course, that required a signature. Unable to move any part of his body except his head, he wondered how he might sign the card. His mother encouraged him to hold a pen in his mouth. The writing was legible. Later, a friend left some flowers in his room. He attempted to draw, and then paint, flowers. Then, another friend brought a Bible and several books by Ayako Miura to his room. All of these things

—signing the card, painting the flowers, reading the Bible, and reading Miura's books—contributed to his new happiness.

5 BIBLE FOR GLOBAL LITERACY

"Come to me, all you who are weary and burdened, and I will give you rest." (Matthew 11:28 [NIV])

「疲れた者，重荷を負う者は，だれでもわたしのもとに来なさい。休ませてあげよう。」
（マタイによる福音書 11 章 28 節）

　これもイエス・キリストの言葉です。宗教は人を縛るものと考えられている場合がありますが，この聖書の言葉は逆に，イエス・キリストのもとに真の精神的な自由と休息があると教えています。

　READING SECTION に登場する星野富弘さんの初期の作品の一つに，「空（かりんの実）」があります。その詩画には「恐る恐る開いた　マタイの福音書　あの時から　空が変わった」とあります。不慮の事故に遭い，病院のベッドに横たわっていた星野さんのもとに，知り合いが一冊の聖書を届けてくれたそうです。始めて開いたのが，新約聖書の冒頭にある『マタイによる福音書』だったのでしょうか。その後，星野さんは聖書から得た様々な教えをヒントに多くの詩画を生み出してきました。

　世界の人々が読んでいる聖書ですが，聖書のどの言葉を特に好むかは人によってもちろん異なります。また，国や文化，時代等の違いによって好まれる聖書の言葉も違ってくるようです。現代日本で最も好まれている聖書の言葉の一つは上記の言葉であるとよく言われるのですが，そのことは何を示唆しているのでしょうか。

6 CULTURAL NOTES

　ふるさと創生事業により1991年春に，星野富弘氏の作品を公開する富弘美術館が，星野氏のふるさと群馬県みどり市東町に誕生しました。美術館のホームページには，次のように紹介されています。「四季折々の野の草花やシャクナゲの群生，紅キリシマツツジの大木など，青空と緑深い詩情豊かな山々に囲まれた東村。不慮の事故での9年間の入院生活から久しぶりにふるさとに帰った星野さんを迎えたのは，子どもの頃から慣れ親しんだそんな東村の自然でした。でもそれは，初めて見るような美しさだったといいます。星野さんを見守り，育んだ，やさしく厳しい東村の自然。東村のそんな美しい自然の中にとけこむように建っています。」　星野氏の作品（詩）には，美しい花が添えられています。深い余韻を残す詩と癒しに満ちた水彩画を見ると，心がリセットされるような気持になります。(https://www.city.midori.gunma.jp/www/contents/1389160237278/index.html)

7 READING SECTION NOTES

l. 2.　manure　肥料
l. 3.　fertilize　肥沃にする　　cf. fertilizer　肥料
l.10.　paralyzed　麻痺した
l.11.　burdened　苦しむ
l.19.　haul　（重い荷物を）運ぶ

8 LECTURE NOTES

l. 2.　accomplished　熟練した
l. 2.　collaborator　協力者
l. 2.　cultivate　磨く
l. 5.　maneuver　手順
l. 6.　vaulting　跳躍
l. 8.　episode　出来事，エピソード
l. 8.　attribute to ～　　～のおかげであると考える
l.16.　legible　判読可能な

Tomihiro Hoshino experienced a great change in his life. Once he had been strong. In fact, he became a junior high school physical education teacher, but he suffered a terrible accident while teaching. He became paralyzed. For nine years, his mother took care of him in the hospital. The Reading Section says that he suffered guilt and depression; he felt sorry that his mother had to do so much for him. One day, his hospital roommate had to be transferred. Tomihiro wanted to sign a farewell card, but he could only move his head. His mother suggested that he hold a pen in his mouth and sign the card. Then a visitor brought him some flowers. He drew pictures of the flowers. He got married, he studied the Bible, and he enjoyed books by Ayako Miura. The Reading Section says he is a respected artist with his own museum in Azuma Village. He has exhibitions in New York and other big cities. Hoshino has progressed from depression to happiness.

10 CHRISTIANITY AROUND YOU

<Cross and Crucifix 十字架と十字架像>

The Christian Cross represents the sacrificial death of Jesus Christ. Tomihiro Hoshino describes his first sight of a cross at a gravesite. Later, he became a Christian. Another person who was interested in the Cross is Henry Dunant, the Swiss founder of the International Red Cross, a disaster relief organization. In Protestant churches, the cross is the simple cross-bar design. In Catholic churches crucifixes have the body of Christ attached. Throughout the world, crosses are symbols of caring. The Green Cross is the international symbol of hospitals, and the Blue Cross symbolizes a popular medical insurance.

Chapter 15 / *Maria Callas*

1 READING SECTION

Read the following passage for 3 minutes.

Maria Callas was a world-famous opera singer. Often recognized as one of the most influential soprano singers of the twentieth century, she was particularly famous for her roles in *Tosca, La Traviata* and *Norma.* She was also a beautiful woman, and some people compared her to the beautiful actress, Audrey Hepburn. 5

In the midst of her successful career, Maria was involved in a romantic affair. As a result, she began losing interests in opera performances. When asked why she wouldn't perform, Maria said, "No man (no one) can serve two masters." She meant that she was choosing romance over opera, as she could not have the two at the same time. 10

"No one can serve two masters," were actually words of Jesus Christ in the Bible. Jesus was not talking about opera versus romance. He was talking about loving God versus loving money. The words originally meant that making money was less important than serving God, or the greater good. In other words, Jesus was talking about the 15 importance of setting priorities.

Money can be used to serve the greater good. Bill Gates, the founder of Microsoft, has joined 150 billionaires who signed *The Giving Pledge*. They promise to give away most of their money. Recently, Robert F. Smith, a wealthy businessman, surprised the world. He 20 was the 2019 graduation speaker at Morehouse College in Atlanta,

Georgia. During the speech he suddenly announced he was paying the student loans of the 400 graduates. These two men used their money to benefit the world.

2 LISTENING SECTION

Listen to a lecture on the topic you just read about.

3 QUESTION (SUMMARY)

Summarize the points made in the lecture, being sure to explain how the Reading Section deepens the understanding of the lecture passage (125 to 175 words). You have 20 minutes to plan and write your response.

4 LECTURE TRANSCRIPT

Maria Callas was born in New York in 1923, as a descendent of Greek immigrants to the United States. Her family life was complicated. Her mother and father only agreed on one thing: Maria had a great voice. Unfortunately, the parents did not have a loving relationship. Maria competed with her older sister, Jackie, for their parent's love. Jackie was beautiful. 5 Maria struggled with weight problems most of her life. The mother, Evangelia, decided that Maria should be an opera singer. She also decided that Jackie, would marry a rich, Greek man. To achieve these goals, Evangelia returned to Greece with her two daughters.

Maria studied music in Athens, Greece. She made her debut as an opera 10 singer in 1938. With her beautiful voice and energetic performances, Maria quickly became a success on the stage. Her life, however, was not always devoted to music alone. She fell in love with Aristotle Onassis. He was a famous Greek shipping magnate and an international playboy.

As a result, Maria began performing in fewer operas. She was enjoying   15
her romance and socializing with famous people. By saying, "no man can
serve two masters," she was talking about her decision to make her music
less important than her romance.

Unfortunately, Aristotle Onassis left Maria after two years. That affair ended when Onassis became fascinated with Jacqueline Kennedy, the widow of   20
the late President John F. Kennedy. When he married Jacqueline, Maria's
heart was broken.

5 BIBLE FOR GLOBAL LITERACY

**"No one can serve two masters. Either you will hate the one and love the other,
or you will be devoted to the one and despise the other. You cannot serve both
God and money." (Matthew 6:24 [NIV])**

「だれも，二人の主人に仕えることはできない。一方を憎んで他方を愛するか，一方に親
しんで他方を軽んじるか，どちらかである。あなたがたは，神と富とに仕えることはで
きない。」（マタイによる福音書6章24節）

　「新約聖書」には，イエス・キリストの生涯と教えを記した四つの『福音書』，教会の始まりを記
した『使徒言行録』，そして信仰に関する教えが記された多数の書簡（手紙）が含まれます。漢訳聖
書を元にした「福音書」という名称は分かりづらいかもしれません。英語では「福音書」のことを
The Gospels（「ゴスペル」の語源），または The Good News（良い知らせ）と言います。この方が
分かりやすいでしょうか。

　上記の言葉は，マタイという弟子が記したイエス・キリストの生涯と教えである『マタイによる
福音書』の一節で，イエス・キリストの言葉の引用です。神を信じることと，お金を第一とするこ
とが対比されているのですが，ここでおもしろいのは「主人に仕える」という封建主義的な比喩が
用いられている点です。お金を第一とする生き方は，いつの間にか自分をお金に従属させている生
き方ではないか，という示唆がここに見てとれます。

　一方，「誰も二人の主人に仕えることはできない」という言葉は，二者択一が迫られている状況
を表す言葉として，西洋で広く用いられてきました。マリア・カラスも，そのような一般的な意味
でこの言葉を用いています。聖書の元の意味から離れて，その言葉自体が一人歩きすることも多い
のです。

6 CULTURAL NOTES

　オペラは，男女の愛憎劇などを歌にのせて表現する芸術です。マリア・カラスは声楽技術に加えて感情表現に人一倍長けており，実生活での恋愛や，当時の一般通念的なオペラ歌手のイメージと異なる，美貌と容姿で一世を風靡しました。しかし，ピアノやヴァイオリンのような楽器ではなく，声帯という人間に備わった器官を使い表現するため，その維持には大変な努力が必要であったようです。

　マリア・カラスの当たり役であった『トスカ』『椿姫』『ノルマ』などは，ソプラノ歌手としての技量が試されるもので，特にベッリーニの『ノルマ』中の有名なアリア「清らかな女神よ」は，難易度が高く喉への負担が大きいため，これを避けるソプラノ歌手は多いと言われます。カラスは，このアリアを誰よりも多く，完璧に歌ったといわれています。

7 READING SECTION NOTES

l. 2.　influential　影響を及ぼす

l. 2.　soprano　ソプラノ（の）

8 LECTURE NOTES

l.10.　debut　デビューする

l.20.　fascinated with　〜に心を奪われる

l.20.　widow　未亡人

9 SUMMARY SAMPLE

Although Maria Callas achieved great success as an opera singer, her life had moments of sadness. She was born in New York, but her homelife was not happy. Her parents did not get on well, and Maria and her sister competed for their parents' attention. Additionally, Maria struggled with her weight when she was young. The mother decided to move with her daughters to Greece so that Maria could have a better chance in opera. She became a famous star. The Reading Section describes her as a beautiful woman. Aristotle Onassis, the rich businessman, fell in love with her. She began spending less time with her music and more time with him. She made up her mind that her love affair was more important. Unfortunately, Onassis married Jacqueline Kennedy. Callas was heartbroken.

\<Beethoven, Haydn, Bernstein—Composers of the Mass ミサ・ミサ曲(ベートーヴェン，ハイドン，バーンスタイン)>

The Mass is a very formal religious service honoring the life of Jesus Christ. It is performed daily in Catholic churches although Sunday attendance is an obligation for Catholics. The same prayers are recited at all masses. On very special occasions (called high masses), these prayers are sung, often in Latin. Through the centuries, famous composers have set the mass to music. The masses of Bach, Beethoven, and Haydn have been performed in churches, museums, and concert halls. Many of the people in the audiences may not be religious at all, but they respond to the great beauty. The most famous modern mass is Leonard Bernstein's *Mass: A Theatre Piece for Singers, Players and Dancers*. It was commissioned by Jacqueline Kennedy in honor of her late husband. Bernstein was Jewish and his masterpiece is an inspiration to people of all backgrounds.

1 READING SECTION

Read the following passage for 3 minutes.

In 2014 Dr. Kent Brantly suddenly showed up in world-wide media after contracting the Ebola virus while serving as a humanitarian aid medical doctor in Liberia, West Africa. Contracting Ebola was a "death sentence" at the time. Brantly was soon sent to Emory Hospital in Atlanta, Georgia for treatment. From his bed at Emory, he 5 recalled an ancient story of the suffering people of Israel in the Bible.

The story is nearly 3,000 years old. It concerns the people of Israel who were conquered by the Babylonian empire. It was a bitter experience for them to accept the demands of the foreign government. One of the demands of the Babylonians was that the people of Israel 10 had to bow down before a golden statue. Three men refused to obey. Their punishment was to be thrown into a fiery furnace. Just before entering the flames they said: "If we are thrown into the blazing furnace, the God we serve is able to save us ... but even if he does not, we ... will not (obey you)." 15

Dr. Brantly quoted those words during the uncertainty of his recovery. They helped him to be brave fighting Ebola. He believed he was protected by a greater power that could rid him of the disease. Brantly especially liked the phrase, "even if." Even if he were not cured of the Ebola, he still believed that his humanitarian work was worthwhile. 20

2 LISTENING SECTION

Listen to a lecture on the topic you just read about.

3 QUESTION (SUMMARY)

Summarize the points made in the lecture, being sure to explain how the Reading Section deepens the understanding of the lecture passage (125 to 175 words). You have 20 minutes to plan and write your response.

4 LECTURE TRANSCRIPT

Dr. Kent Brantly is an American doctor who moved with his wife and two children to Liberia, West Africa in 2013. He was part of a team sent for humanitarian aid. Their purpose was to relieve the suffering in the region. Within a few months, the Ebola virus raged throughout the area. Brantly sent his family back to Texas. On the day that he drove his family to the 5 airport in Africa, he fell ill. It was soon discovered that he contracted Ebola. The medical staff in Liberia offered him an experimental drug. He declined the drug, insisting that a fellow worker, who had also contracted Ebola, should be given first access to the drug.

Finally, Brantly was transported to Emory University Hospital in Georgia. 10 Although he is American, many people protested his return. They were fearful that the disease would spread in the United States. Dr. Brantly went through an intense treatment. After a few months, he did recover.

Throughout his life, Brantly had been nurtured in an environment that taught him the importance of serving others. He grew up in a family that 15 constantly attended churches. He enjoyed going to Christian summer camps and to a Christian university. His background taught him to live unselfishly. Although some friends were nervous about him going to Africa, they realized that kindness and generosity were keys to his nature. Those

qualities caused him to be chosen as the TIME Magazine Person of the
Year in 2014.

5 BIBLE FOR GLOBAL LITERACY

"If we are thrown into the blazing furnace, the God we serve is able to deliver us from it, and he will deliver us from Your Majesty's hand. **But even if he does not,** we want you to know, Your Majesty, that **we will not** serve your gods or worship the image of gold you have set up." (**Daniel 3:17-18 [NIV]**)

　※太字部分が上記 **READING SECTION** での引用部分。

「わたしたちのお仕えする神は，その燃え盛る炉や王様の手からわたしたちを救うことが
できますし，必ず救ってくださいます。そうでなくとも，御承知ください。わたしたち
は王様の神々に仕えることも，お建てになった金の像を拝むことも，決していたしませ
ん。」（ダニエル書 3 章 17 節-18 節）

　旧約聖書『ダニエル書』は，古代イスラエルのユダ王国が新バビロニア帝国の侵略を受けて崩壊
し，ユダの人々の一部がバビロニア帝国に強制的に連行された物語を背景としています。バビロニ
ア帝国では，金の像を拝まない者は火刑に処されるという理不尽な御触れが出されます。圧倒的な
権力を前にしたユダの人々は，それでも金の像を拝みません。例え困難がその先にあると分かって
いても，正しいと信じる道を選択する。それが，ユダの人々が示した姿勢でした。ちなみに，この
物語の続きでは，燃える炉の中でユダの人々が奇跡的に天使に守られる様が描かれます。
　大日本帝国統治下の朝鮮半島では，神社参拝が強要されました。その際，学校の教師であった安
利淑は，キリスト教信仰をもとに参拝を拒否し，厳しい迫害を受けました。迫害や危険を顧みずに
自分が正しいと信じる道を貫いた彼女の手記は，後に『たといそうでなくても』とのタイトルで日
本でも出版されました。ここにも，『ダニエル書』の言葉に導かれた人の姿勢が見てとれます。

6 CULTURAL NOTES

　エボラ出血熱は，主として患者の体液等（血液，分泌物，吐物・排泄物）に触れることによりウイルス感染する疾病です。これまでに，アフリカ中央部のコンゴ民主共和国，スーダン，ウガンダ，ガボンやアフリカ西部のギニア，リベリア，シエラレオネ，マリ，ナイジェリア，コートジボワールで発生しています。2014 年 3 月以降，ギニア，リベリア，シエラレオネ，マリ，ナイジェリアでエボラ出血熱の大規模流行が発生しました。発症は突発的で，症状は発熱，倦怠感，食欲低下，頭痛など。その後嘔吐，下痢，腹痛などの消化器症状が見られます。致死率はウイルスによって異なりますが，高いものだと 80-90%と報告されています（厚生労働省 HP）。

7 READING SECTION NOTES

l. 2.　Ebola virus　エボラウイルス

l. 2.　humanitarian aid　人道的な援助

l. 4.　death sentence　致命的病気　死刑宣告

l. 8.　Babylonian empire　バビロニア帝国

l.12.　fiery furnace　燃え盛る炉

8 LECTURE NOTES

l. 4.　rage　猛威を振るう

l.14.　nurture　養育する

l.17.　unselfishly　無欲に

9 SUMMARY SAMPLE

In 2013, Dr. Kent Brantly, an American doctor from Texas, moved with his wife and children to Liberia, Africa. His purpose was to help the people suffering from Ebola. The disease spread rapidly. Dr. Brantly decided that his family should return to America, but he remained in Africa, hoping to continue his humanitarian work. However, very soon Dr. Brantly, himself contracted the disease. There was a limited supply of an experimental drug, but Dr. Brantly wanted his sick colleague to have first access to the medicine. Finally, he was sent to a hospital in America for treatment. Many American people did not want him to enter the country. They were fearful that Ebola would kill people there. Two points in the Reading Section show Brantly's good character: he was aware that Ebola was considered a "death sentence," and he still believed his humanitarian work in Liberia was worthwhile. The Lecture explains that his family, his church, and his university had taught him to be unselfish.

10 CHRISTIANITY AROUND YOU

<Christian Health Care　キリスト教と医療>

Throughout the centuries Christians have attended to the sick. Father Damien (1840-1889), a Belgian Catholic priest, worked in the leper colony in Hawaii. Eventually, he himself, caught the disease and died in the colony. Dr. Omalu Bennett is currently serving people in the USA who have suffered concussions. Dr. Kent Brantly of the United States served Ebola sufferers in Liberia, Africa. In Japan, Dr. Shigeaki Hinohara's long life reflects the Christian emphasis on health care. He worked at St. Luke's International Hospital, which has an Episcopal Church background.

1 READING SECTION

Read the following passage for 3 minutes.

Dr. Bennet Omalu is a Nigerian physician living in the United States. He is a critic of American football. He believes it is a dangerous sport, and he has become famous for documenting the brain concussions during the game. Americans are passionate about football. He has upset a large part of American society for speaking negatively [5] about the beloved sport. Naturally, he has made many enemies. In numerous interviews he insists that Americans need to rethink the importance of the sport to society. He believes that many countries have cultural traditions which are not wholesome. For him, football is one of the traditions which should be abandoned. As a dedicated [10] Bible reader, he always keeps a small Bible in his pocket. In a *Los Angeles Times* interview, he read Ephesians 4:22, 24. "You were taught with regard to your former way of life, to put off your old self ... and put on the new self ..."

The passage is a metaphor. It compares changing clothes to changing lifestyles. In the Bible, the writer was primarily talking about [15] getting rid of bad behavior such as gossiping and stealing, etc. But Dr. Omalu was extending the idea to getting rid of cultural traditions which are harmful. Many Americans disapprove of Dr. Omalu. They say he is an outsider who has no authority to suggest change in America. Although football is a money-making business, Dr. Omalu [20] maintains that it is better to be protective of players than to make a profit off of them.

Listen to a lecture on the topic you just read about.

3 QUESTION (SUMMARY)

Summarize the points made in the lecture, being sure to explain how the Reading Section deepens the understanding of the lecture passage (125 to 175 words). You have 20 minutes to plan and write your response.

4 LECTURE TRANSCRIPT

Dr. Bennet Omalu was born in Southeastern Nigeria in 1968. Actually, the family name as it appears here is shortened; the long form of his name translates into English as "He who knows speaks." That is particularly true of the doctor; he has upset American society by denouncing football. He is the discoverer of CTE, the brain disease that is caused by head injuries. 5 When he performed an autopsy on the former football player, Mike Webster, in 2002, he noted brain damage. He acknowledged that some of the damage was due to drug abuse. However, Dr. Omalu indicated that the real damage came from a series of blows to the head.

The National Football League called for Dr. Omalu to retract his published 10 findings. Football is almost a "religion." Some people even skip church on Sundays if there is an important game. The Super Bowl games attract millions of viewers world-wide. For a Nigerian immigrant to speak negatively about the sport was too much for NFL supporters to tolerate. He has said, "No, I do not watch football ... what flashes through my mind is 15 what's going on in their (players') brains."

Dr. Omalu's story has been made into the film, *Concussion*, starring Will

Smith. The discussion of CTE has upset parts of American society. Many poor families regard sports, especially football, as a means for their children to gain college scholarships. Now, some of those parents are looking for other ways for their children and themselves to escape poverty. Dr. Omalu believes they will succeed.

20

5 BIBLE FOR GLOBAL LITERACY

"You were taught, with regard to your former way of life, to put off your old self, ... and to put on the new self ..." (Ephesians 4:22, 24 [NIV])

「… 古い人を脱ぎ捨て，… 新しい人を身に着け …」（エフェソの信徒への手紙4章22節，24節）

　聖書には，隠喩（メタファー）的表現で記されている部分が多くあります。例えば，詩編23編では人間を羊，神を羊飼いに例える隠喩が用いられていることを見ました（3章の**BIBLE FOR GLOBAL LITERACY** 参照）。羊の隠喩には特定の地理的背景があり，日本のように動物園や観光牧場等でしか羊を見ることがない場所に住む人には分かりづらいものでしょう。一方，上記の言葉にある衣服の比喩は，多少わかりやすいでしょうか。

　この言葉は，使徒パウロの名を冠した手紙の一つで，エフェソ（現在のトルコにある都市）やその周辺にいた信者に宛てて書かれたものです。「古い人を脱ぎ捨て，新しい人を身に付ける」という隠喩は，原文ではキリストの真理を受け入れて新しい生き方をすることを意味します。もっとも，この言葉を多様に解釈することもできるでしょう。さなぎから蝶が飛び立つように，思い切って新しい一歩を踏み出すことは，すべての人が時に必要としているのではないでしょうか。

6 CULTURAL NOTES

　アメリカの大手世論調査会社ギャロップが 2017 年に行った調査では，アメリカ人が最も観戦するのが好きなスポーツは，1 位はアメリカンフットボール（37%）です。同年の新聞社の調査では，プロフットボールとカレッジ（大学）フットボールを合わせると約 50% の人が，最も観戦するのが好きなスポーツと答えています。1980 年代は，野球とアメリカンフットボールは同程度の人気でしたが，現在では，アメリカンフットボールがアメリカの国民的スポーツ・娯楽といってよい程の絶大な人気を誇ります。NFL（プロフットボール）王座決定戦であるスーパーボウルは，アメリカ最大のスポーツイベントです。

　大学フットボールでは，元日に開催される，ローズボウル（カリフォルニア州），コットンボウル（テキサス州），シュガーボウル（ルイジアナ州），オレンジボウル（フロリダ州）が「4 大フットボール」と呼ばれる特別な試合です。それぞれの州の特産物の名称がついているのもアメリカらしいと思います。

7 READING SECTION NOTES

l. 1.　Nigerian　ナイジェリア人の

l. 2.　critic　批判する人

l. 3.　document　文書で記録する

l. 3.　brain concussion　脳震とう

l. 4.　passionate　情熱的な

l. 6.　beloved　最愛の

l. 9.　wholesome　有益な

l.10.　dedicated　熱心な

l.17.　get rid of　悪習を断つ，やめる

l.22.　protective　保護用の

8 LECTURE NOTES

l. 4.　denounce　非難する

l. 5.　CTE (chronic traumatic encephalopathy)　慢性外傷性脳症

l. 6.　autopsy　検視

l.10.　retract　取り消す

9 SUMMARY SAMPLE

Dr. Bennet Omalu is a Nigerian doctor who lives in the United States. He has upset many people because he advocates getting rid of American football. He believes it is a dangerous sport. Originally, Dr. Omalu examined the body of Mike Webster, a football player, noting brain injuries. Because football is so important in American culture, there has been strong objection to Omalu's ideas. Both the Reading Section and the Lecture mention that some Americans disapprove of Omalu. The life and struggles of Dr. Omalu are shown in the movie, *Concussion*, starring Will Smith. One problem is that poor families hope their sons can earn university scholarships by playing football. According to Omalu, it is better to be protective of players than to consider the financial gains of football.

10 CHRISTIANITY AROUND YOU

\<Bible 聖書\>

The Bible is a guidebook which many Christians read daily. It is consistently an international bestseller. The Protestant version consists of 66 books. The Catholic collection consists of 73 books. The actual differences in the two versions are minimal, and these days some Catholics and Protestants gather in each other's homes for study. With just a little effort, they can coordinate the pages and passages they want to discuss. The Bible contains, poetry, history, and advice. It was written over a period of 1500 years. Many different writers contributed to it.

Chapter 18 / *Pharrell Williams*

1 READING SECTION

Read the following passage for 3 minutes.

In 2014 Pharrell Williams' hit song *Happy* could be heard everywhere. Williams, an African American hip hop artist, is still a major entertainer. In 2019 Williams appeared at the Academy Awards. Williams was happy to present the award for a category that is dear to his heart. Wearing a dark camouflage tuxedo with short pants, the [5] stylish singer read I Corinthians 13:11 before presenting the award for *The Best Animation Film*: "When I was a child, I talked like a child, I thought like a child, I reasoned like a child. When I became a man, I put childish ways behind me."

Of course, he selected the passage to say that childhood is a special [10] time in life. Animation is specifically designed for delighting children. Williams suggested that animation is one way of bringing joy to children. Williams was actually repeating words used by Paul over two thousand years ago. The passage discusses a transition from childhood to adulthood. There is a time for children to enjoy [15] play, fantasy, and imagination. Children who enjoy these things often grow into successful and well-adjusted adults. David Elkins, author of *The Hurried Child,* speaks against depriving children of sufficient play time. The success of Pharrell Williams and Paul of Tarsus may be attributable to happy childhoods. [20]

2 LISTENING SECTION

Listen to a lecture on the topic you just read about.

3 QUESTION (SUMMARY)

Summarize the points made in the lecture, being sure to explain how the Reading Section deepens the understanding of the lecture passage (125 to 175 words). You have 20 minutes to plan and write your response.

4 LECTURE TRANSCRIPT

Pharrell Williams is a happy man. He was born in Virginia, US, in 1973. He is the writer of the 2014 hit song, *Happy*. Certainly, his life seems to be one good experience after another. He was born into a family that could afford to give him lessons in various musical instruments. While in junior and senior high school, he formed several bands. He attended 5 Northwestern University, but he dropped out after two years to pursue his interest in fashion design, song writing, and film production. He is a success in all of those areas. In 2013, he married his longtime girlfriend. They have a son for whom Williams wrote *Rocket's Theme*. That song was used in the popular *Despicable Me* animation film. Frequently, he appears 10 in award shows, either as a winner or as a presenter.

Fans queue outside of theaters to get a glimpse of him. In addition to composing hit songs, Williams is part owner of the Billionaire Boys Club, a clothing company with offices in New York and Tokyo. He delights everyone with his original fashions. Sometimes he wears very interesting 15 hats. His suits and tuxedos are always unusually designed. He likes to describe himself as a "happy nerd," being original and setting his own style trends.

"When I was a child, I spoke like a child, I thought like a child, I reasoned like a child; when I became an adult, I put an end to childish ways." (I Corinthians 13:11 [NRSV])

「幼子だったとき，わたしは幼子のように話し，幼子のように思い，幼子のように考えていた。成人した今，幼子のことを棄てた。」（コリントの信徒への手紙一 13 章 11 節）

　この言葉もまた，使徒パウロが記した『コリントの信徒への手紙一』の一節です。ここでは，幼子から成人への成長という比喩を通して，人格の成長について述べられています。日本語訳で「幼子のことを棄てた」とある言葉は，英語訳に "I put an end to childish ways." とあるように，「子どもじみたやり方をやめた」というニュアンスの言葉です。つまり，ここで言う「幼さ」は良い意味での「純粋さ」ではなく，大人げなく人間の欲望のみを前面に出してしまうことを意味しています。

　一方，聖書の中では子どもの純粋さが称えられている箇所もあります。例えば，イエスの元に近寄ってきた幼子らを叱った弟子達に対して，イエス・キリストは「子供たちをわたしのところに来させなさい。… 神の国はこのような者たちのものである」（ルカによる福音書 18 章 16 節）と語っています。

6 CULTURAL NOTES

　ファレル・ウィリアムスは，現在アメリカの若者文化のリーダー的存在です。デザイナーと共に設立した「ビリオネアボーイズクラブ」という名前の洋服を中心としたファッション会社は，ポップなデザインを施したアウターやインナーを多く展開していて，日本でもラッパー（ヒップ・ホップ音楽歌手）や若者を中心に人気のブランドとなっています。

　欧米の文化では，イベントやパーティにはドレスコードがあります。タキシードは，招待状にドレスコードとして Formal/Black Tie と記されている場合に男性が着用する正装です。ファレル・ウィリアムスがアカデミー賞のプレゼンターを行った時に着用した迷彩柄の短パンタキシードは，タキシードの通常概念からは逸脱するものです。ファッションアイコンの彼であるからこそ許されるものなのでしょう。

7 READING SECTION NOTES

l. 3.　Academy Awards　アカデミー賞

l. 4.　dear to　〜にとって大切な

l. 5.　camouflage tuxedo　迷彩柄のタキシード

l.11.　delight　楽しませる

l.17.　well-adjusted　社会に適応した

l.20.　attributable to　〜に起因する

8 LECTURE NOTES

l.10.　*Despicable Me*　映画の邦題「怪盗グルーの月泥棒」
　　　despicable　見下げ果てた

l.12.　queue　列を作る

l.12.　get a glimpse of　一目見る

l.17.　nerd　オタク

Pharrell Williams' hit song, *Happy*, reflects his good life. He grew up in a family that could provide him with music lessons. During middle school and high school, he formed his own bands. Later, he attended college, but he dropped out so that he could devote time to music and fashion. He became very successful. According to the Reading Section he showed up at the 2019 Academy Awards wearing a camouflage-design tuxedo. The Lecture says that fans stand outside of theaters just so they can see what he is wearing. He is a partner of the Billionaire Boys Club which has offices in New York and Tokyo. *Happy* is the perfect title for Williams' song because he enjoys so many good things.

Chapter 19 / *Prince William*

1 READING SECTION

Read the following passage for 3 minutes.

On May 22, 2017, there was a terror attack at the Manchester Arena in the United Kingdom. Near the end of an Ariana Grande concert, a bomb exploded. Most of the concert-goers were young people who had come to hear the American singer. Police reported that there were 22 fatalities and 139 casualties. One year later, Prince William [5] attended a memorial service at the Manchester Cathedral; his reading of I Corinthians 13 is considered one of the most polished public readings. Judging by the number of visitors to the YouTube site, Prince William has further distinguished himself as a man possessed of a wonderful –and consoling voice. His diction was perfect. He [10] managed to read the extended passage while looking up at intervals to fasten his eyes on the people. He wanted to convey his sincerity.

I Corinthians 13 is often recited at weddings and at funerals. The theme is love. Among the many verses in the passage are the familiar words: "Love is patient, love is kind. It does not envy, it does not [15] boast. It is not proud. It is not rude."

Prince William could read those words convincingly because he has a reputation for those qualities. Before he entered St. Andrews University, he spent a year getting acquainted with people in Chile, England, Kenya, and other countries. While doing volunteer work, he [20] impressed his fellow workers with his good personality and willingness to "carry his own load." There is a photo online showing him scrubbing the bathroom floor near the toilet. He didn't demand special treatment. Obviously, such an attitude would win him many friends.

Many people attest to the Prince's consistent patience and kindness. When he escorted his wife and new-born son from the hospital in 2013, he paused for a few minutes to answer the usual questions from the crowd. Finally, he wiped his brow with his rolled-up shirtsleeves and drove himself and his family home. Prince William exemplifies the message of I Corinthians 13; good people, no matter how important they are, take time to focus on others.

2 LISTENING SECTION

Listen to a lecture on the topic you just read about.

3 QUESTION (SUMMARY)

Summarize the points made in the lecture, being sure to explain how the Reading Section deepens the understanding of the lecture passage (150 to 225 words). You have 20 minutes to plan and write your response.

4 LECTURE TRANSCRIPT

Prince William was born in 1982, the son of Princess Diana and Prince Charles. He is the grandson of Queen Elizabeth II. Humorously, he informed his mother when he was only seven years old that he intended to be a policeman one day; such a profession would allow him to protect her. Perhaps he was already aware of the harassment of the press. Sadly, the hounding of tabloid reporters caused Diana's death in a car accident. Despite that tragic event, William grew up to be a man of many talents.

Throughout high school and university, he did well in his studies and in sports. He excelled in geography, and he performed well in polo, swimming, and basketball. Before entering St. Andrews University, he spent an adventurous "gap year." Even though he was born into privilege, he used that time to form friendships with ordinary people. He did army training in Belize, worked on dairy farms in England, taught children in Chile, and did volunteer work in Africa. His enjoyable time in Africa prompted him to learn Swahili. People in those places were impressed that the Prince did not depend on servants; he did his own chores, even taking his turn cleaning the bathroom. His eagerness to learn makes him a popular future king.

After completing military training in 2006, William was made an officer in the Royal Army. However, the government decided that he should not get involved in combat. Subsequently, William spent time in the Royal Navy and the Royal Air Force. For two years, he served as an air ambulance pilot. He donated all of his salary to various charities.

Prince William married Catherine Middleton in Westminster Abbey in London on April 29, 2011. He, his wife, and their three children often walk in public, cheerfully greeting admirers. People respond to his social skills, especially his smile and his perfect English diction. His reading of I Corinthians 13, a Bible passage, on YouTube, is a frequently watched video. William of Cambridge is a gifted sportsman, student of cultures, and an articulate prince.

"Love is patient, love is kind. It does not envy, it does not boast, it is not proud. It does not dishonor others ..." (I Corinthians 13:4-5 [NIV])

「愛は忍耐強い。愛は情け深い。ねたまない。愛は自慢せず，高ぶらない。礼を失せず…」（コリントの信徒への手紙一 13 章 4 節-5 節）

　愛の崇高さについて記されているこの言葉は，『コリントの信徒への手紙一』にある使徒パウロの言葉です。この手紙の 13 章は「愛の章句」として知られ，西洋だけでなく日本のキリスト教式結婚式でも良く読まれるものです。もっとも，本来ここで語られている愛は男女のロマンスではなく，すべての他者に対して持つべき精神に他なりません。「愛」という言葉を，「他者を何よりも大切にすること」と言い換えても良いかもしれません。

　上記の言葉に続いて，パウロは愛について次のようにも記しています――「（愛は）自分の利益を求めず，いらだたず，恨みを抱かない。不義を喜ばず，真実を喜ぶ。すべてを忍び，すべてを信じ，すべてを望み，すべてに耐える」（同書 13 章 5-7 節）。このような愛の精神を，夫婦間だけでなく全ての人との関係において持つことはもちろん簡単ではありません。だからこそパウロは，そのような愛を「追い求め（続け）なさい」（同書 14 章 1 節）とも記しているのです。

6 CULTURAL NOTES

　ウィリアム王子が大学進学前に 1 年間をかけて世界各地でボランティア活動を行った制度は，「ギャップイヤー」，または長期学外学修プログラムと呼ばれる英国発祥の制度で，休学中に様々な活動や留学，旅行で見聞を広めることが想定されています。大学卒業後の大学院進学前や就職前に適用されることもあります。2016 年にオバマ前大統領の長女がハーバード大学進学を 1 年延期してキャップイヤーを採ったことでアメリカでも認知度が高まりました。日本においても，2014 年

に文部科学省が「学事暦の多様化とギャップイヤーを活用した学外学修プログラムの推進に向けて」（意見のまとめ）で，「ギャップイヤーを経験した学生は，未経験の学生に比べて高い教育的効果が上がっている。」と報告し，現在日本の大学でも「ギャップイヤープログラム」が導入されている大学もあります。

7 READING SECTION NOTES

l.10.　consoling　慰めをもたらすような

l.10.　diction　話し方

l.26.　attest to　～（人，物）を証明する

8 LECTURE NOTES

l. 6.　hound　しつこく追いかける

l. 6.　tabloid　タブロイド版新聞

l. 9.　excel in　（学業に）優れている

l.28.　William of Cambridge　ケンブリッジ公ウィリアム

9 SUMMARY SAMPLE

Both the Reading Section and the Lecture describe Prince William of the United Kingdom as a man who has excellent social skills. In high school and in university, he was successful in his studies while he enjoyed sports. During the year between high school and university, he traveled to various countries. In one picture, he is on his hands and knees scrubbing the floor very near the toilet. He impressed people in Kenya and Chile, living among them as an ordinary man; he did his own chores. Further, his interest in Africa led him to study Swahili. Later, he entered the Army, but the government decided that he should not be a combat soldier; instead, he spent periods in the Royal Air Force and Royal Navy. At one point, he piloted an air ambulance.

Not only did the prince downplay his royal status during that gap year, he continues to take opportunities to avoid pageantry and ceremony. The Reading Section describes the scene of the Prince when he appeared at the hospital to take his wife and new-born son home. He was dressed in rolled-up shirtsleeves when he came out of the hospital to greet well-wishers. After exchanging the usual small talk with the public, he personally drove his family home.

10 CHRISTIANITY AROUND YOU

<Baptism 洗礼>

Prince George, son of the Prince William and Duchess Kate, was born on July 22, 2013. He was baptized on October 23, 2013. Different churches have different styles of baptism; the royal family are members of the Church of England. That church is among the group of churches which practice infant baptism. In that style, a priest pours a small amount of water over the head of the child. It marks the child's acceptance into the Christian faith. Godparents take part in the ceremony, and they promise to watch over the child's development in the event the parents are not able to do so. Usually, there are just two godparents. In the case of Prince George, there were seven godparents. The event was held in the Royal Chapel of Buckingham Palace. Some churches reserve baptism only for adults. Whether infant baptism or adult baptism, the event usually involves water. In the case of adults, it can be done in the river or in the ocean, or in an inside pool. Justin Bieber was baptized in his friend's bathtub in 2015.

Chapter 20 / *Mahatma Gandhi*

1 READING SECTION

Read the following passage for 3 minutes.

Mohandas Gandhi lived in the 20th century and is well-known for his campaigns for civil rights in India and South Africa. Portraits of Mohandas (or Mahatma) Gandhi are instantly recognizable. His pictures show him as a very thin man, wearing the simple white cloth. Most often his shoulders are bare. His dark eyes are encircled by wire-framed glasses. He was born in India in 1869, and he died in his beloved country in 1948. Yet these many years later, people still recognize him as "The Father of India." 5

Gandhi was a lawyer. He dedicated himself to liberating peasants in South Africa and India. He was a deeply spiritual man. He was well-read in the literature of the Hindus, the Sikhs, and the Muslims. Most interestingly, he studied the Christian Bible and was particularly impressed with the words of Jesus Christ, especially Matthew 5: 39: "But I tell you, do not resist an evil person. If someone strikes you on the right cheek, turn to him the other also." 10 15

Those well-known words are the basis of non-violent protest. They are embedded in *The Sermon on the Mount*. Jesus spoke those words over two thousand years ago. Gandhi, never a Christian, realized that this message would be useful in forcing British occupiers to "Quit India." Gandhi believed that oppressors might become ashamed of themselves for abusing people who do not fight back. Some people 20 would say that the non-violence of Jesus, and later Gandhi, is not realistic. Powerful people might never limit their own power. But there is another element that could force oppressors to give up their meanness. News photographs of the mistreatment can project the image of the mean bully. Public opinion often forces bullies to stop their abuse. In 1947, Britain did grant independence to India.

Although he remained impressed with the teachings of Jesus, Gandhi harshly criticized modern Christians. He loved the gentleness of Jesus; he objected to the greed and aggressive behavior of <u>some</u> Christians.

2 LISTENING SECTION

Listen to a lecture on the topic you just read about.

3 QUESTION (SUMMARY)

Summarize the points made in the lecture, being sure to explain how the Reading Section deepens the understanding of the lecture passage (150 to 225 words). You have 20 minutes to plan and write your response.

4 LECTURE TRANSCRIPT

Mohandas (or Mahatma) Gandhi was born in 1869 in India. He campaigned against British control of both India and South Africa. He popularized the modern non-violent protest movement which involved refusing to physically attack oppressors. He even became angry with his own countrymen when they protested against the British in 1919. He insisted that Indian people refrain from attacking British people. Instead, he believed that they should burn their own British clothing and boycott British goods. He thought that an economic protest would cause the British to rethink their colonial policies. Naturally, many Indians could not understand Gandhi's emphasis on love and peace.

Gandhi was a spiritual man, well-read in the scriptures of the Sikhs and Hindus. He even read the Christian Bible. A favorite Bible passage for him was *The Sermon on the Mount,* in which Jesus Christ denounces violence. Gandhi was no Christian. In fact he complained about the behavior of many people who called themselves Christians but who behaved in unkind ways. Still, he appreciated the words of Jesus and practiced a simple life. He began fasting. He denied himself food for long periods, causing him to appear painfully thin in photos. Although he was an educated lawyer, Gandhi lived like the poor peasants around him. He gave up wearing suits and hats, and took up the white loincloth which he, himself, made on a loom. Once, he attended a peace conference with British negotiators. They offered him a room in an expensive hotel; Gandhi declined the luxurious accommodation. Instead he stayed in a very cheap room. He would never relent to British occupation, and he insisted on the slogan "Quit India."

While on his way to a prayer meeting in 1948, Gandhi was assassinated by a Hindu nationalist. Even though many Indians did not subscribe to the idea of non-violence during his lifetime, Gandhi is regarded with great affection today. He is commonly referred to as "Bapu" or Father. His birthday, October 2, is a national holiday in India.

"But I tell you, do not resist an evil person. If anyone slaps you on the right cheek, turn to them the other cheek also." (Matthew 5:39 [NIV])

「しかし，わたしは言っておく。悪人に手向かってはならない。だれかがあなたの右の頬を打つなら，左の頬をも向けなさい。」（マタイによる福音書 5 章 39 節）

　上記の言葉は「山上の説教」として知られるイエス・キリストの教えの一部で，この後に「敵を愛し，自分を迫害する者のために祈りなさい」（同書 5 章 44 節）という言葉が続いています。これらの言葉は，イエスの教えが徹底した平和主義であったことを示唆しています。（しかし，紀元 4 世紀に国家権力と結び付いて以来，西洋のキリスト教は大勢として戦争を肯定するようになってしまいます。）

　インド独立の父と呼ばれるガンディーは，ヒンドゥー教の教えだけでなく「山上の説教」やトルストイの教えからも学んでイギリスに対する非暴力・不服従の運動を進めました。そのガンディーの姿勢は，米国における人種差別撤廃のためにキング牧師が進めた非暴力主義の運動にも影響を与えています。

　ちなみに，平和の象徴として知られる「オリーブの葉を咥えた鳩」のイメージは，旧約聖書『創世記』にある「ノアの箱舟物語」内のエピソードに由来しています。この物語では洪水という災難が起こるのですが，雨が止んでしばらくした後に鳩がオリーブの葉を咥えて箱舟に戻って来ます。そのことによって，災難（洪水）が過ぎ去ったこと，つまり平和が回復したことが表されているのです。

6 CULTURAL NOTES

　インドの主な宗教はヒンドゥー教，国民の約80％がヒンドゥー教徒です。ヒンドゥー教は多神教で，カースト制度を生んだ宗教としても知られます。牛が神格化されていることでも有名です。次に信者が多いのがイスラム教で，13.4％を占めます。インドというとステレオタイプ的にターバンを巻いた人が描かれることがありますが，ターバンを巻いているのは，髪や髭を切ってはいけないという掟を守っているシク教徒で，人口の約2％です。そのほかにも，キリスト教徒，仏教，ゾロアスター教（拝火教）の信者もいます。https://bharatmemo.com/india-culture-religion-summary

7 READING SECTION NOTES

l. 5.　encircle　取り囲む
l. 6.　wire-framed　ワイヤーフレームの
l.11.　the Hindus　ヒンドゥー教徒
l.11.　the Sikhs　シク教徒
l.11.　the Muslims　ムスリム教徒
l.17.　embed　埋め込む
l.19.　"Quit India"　ガンジーがイギリスに対し，「インドから出て行け」と要求した反英大衆運動
l.20.　oppressor　圧制者
l.21.　abuse　虐待する
l.27.　grant independence　独立を認める

8 LECTURE NOTES

l. 2.　popularize　世に広める
l.20.　loincloth　腰巻
l.21.　loom　織機
l.24.　relent to　〜に屈する
l.27.　subscribe　同意する
l.29.　Bapu　ヒンディー語で「父」の意味

According to the Lecture, Mohandas Gandhi was a spiritual man. Though he was a trained lawyer, he identified with the poor people of India and South Africa. He ate simply and wore a simple cloth which he made himself on a loom. He campaigned for the civil rights of peasants and popularized the non-violent protest idea. During one occasion in India, Gandhi cautioned Indian people against attacking the British. He preferred to use economic boycott as a means of protests. Further, he encouraged Indians to burn their British-made clothing. Understandably, Gandhi did not convince all of his countrymen to follow his method of protests. He read the scriptures of many different religions, and he emphasized peace and love. The Reading Section says that although Gandhi was not a Christian, he liked the ideas of Jesus in *The Sermon on the Mount*. Ironically, while he was on his way to a prayer meeting, he was killed by a Hindu nationalist. Today, Gandhi's birthday is a national holiday. He is affectionately known as the Father of India.

1 READING SECTION

Read the following passage for 3 minutes.

The Dalai Lama is the spiritual leader of Tibetan Buddhism. He is respected around the world, and he has commented on various issues which today's global society faces. What threatens world peace, he believes, are various conflicts based on national, racial, and religious differences. When talking with a group of people from the West on the need of people around the world to overcome differences, he quoted the following words:

> 'Who is my mother? Who are my brothers?' and looking around at those who were sitting in a circle about him he said, 'Here are my mother and brothers. Whoever does the will of God is my brother and sister and mother.'

These words come from the Bible, and the speaker ("he") is Jesus Christ. The Buddhist leader believes there is something we all should learn from these words. In this story, Jesus Christ was with a large group of people. His own mother and brothers could not get near him. Some people told him that his family wanted to speak with him. Then Jesus said the above words, implying that he accepts anyone ("whoever does the will of God") as his "family."

As the Dalai Lama was quick to understand, Jesus was teaching that society will progress when all people accept their connectedness to all other human beings. Of course, DNA relationships are important, but too many people limit their love to their specific family or tribe. The lesson in this story is not to minimize our actual mothers, brothers and sisters, but to appreciate all human beings as members of the larger, human family.

Human beings continue to be tribal—only appreciating their own family, culture, or country. As a Buddhist who believes in the gradual enlightenment of human beings, the Dalai Lama recognized that Jesus was expressing an ideal of universal brotherhood.

2 LISTENING SECTION

Listen to a lecture on the topic you just read about.

3 QUESTION (SUMMARY)

Summarize the points made in the lecture, being sure to explain how the Reading Section deepens the understanding of the lecture passage (150 to 225 words). You have 20 minutes to plan and write your response.

4 LECTURE TRANSCRIPT

Tenzin Gyatso, better known as His Holiness the Fourteenth Dalai Lama, is respected for his joyful personality and his frequent visits with people of different religious backgrounds. Born into a poor family in Northeastern Tibet on July 6, 1935, he passed a series of tests and was installed as the Dalai Lama two years later. He enjoys sharing ideas. He doesn't believe people should abandon their particular religion and change to another. For him, the world is beautiful when people adhere to the religious traditions of their culture.

In 1994, the Dalai Lama was invited to address a group of Christian leaders at a seminar. The Christian hosts asked him to read aloud passages of the Bible and to give his own interpretation as a Buddhist. He greeted his audience as "spiritual brothers and sisters." When he read the Christian Bible passages and shared his Buddhist interpretation with them, everyone (of all religious backgrounds) felt inspired.

He travels in order to show respect. He visited Memphis in the United States in 2009 so that he could pay homage to the late Martin Luther King, Jr. The Dalai Lama spoke softly and expressed his appreciation of the Civil Rights Movement. He referred to Dr. King's famous *I Have a Dream* speech and spoke of his own dream of Tibetan liberation. His charm is his ability to identify with others. When he visited Hiroshima in 2010, the Dalai Lama praised the Japanese for their remarkable recovery from World War II. He said, "You have suffered greatly, but you rebuilt your nation into a modern, peaceful and highly developed nation." Then, typically, he smiled and joked: "Now, to go globally, you need to learn English." Of course, he always laughs at his own poor English ability.

5 BIBLE FOR GLOBAL LITERACY

"And he replied, 'Who are my mother and my brothers?' And looking at those who sat around him, he said, 'Here are my mother and my brothers! Whoever does the will of God is my brother and sister and mother.'" (Mark 3:33-35 [NRSV])

「イエスは，『わたしの母，わたしの兄弟とはだれか』と答え，周りに座っている人々を見回して言われた。『見なさい。ここにわたしの母，わたしの兄弟がいる。神の御心を行う人こそ，わたしの兄弟，姉妹，また母なのだ。』」(マルコによる福音書3章33節-35節)

聖書の言葉をキリスト教徒ではない人が肯定的に取り上げることは，世界の中では決して珍しくありません。さらに言えば，キリスト教徒以外の人が，キリスト教徒以上に聖書の言葉の意味を深く理解していることもあり得るのです。**READING SECTION** に記されているチベット仏教指導者ダライ・ラマによる上記の言葉の引用は，まさにそのことを示唆しています。

　キリスト教徒と他宗教の信者が対立する悲劇は，現代に至るまで何度も繰り返されてきました。十字軍のように，キリスト教の名のもとに行われた殺戮によって多くのイスラム教徒の命が奪われ，結果的にキリスト教と他宗教の間に禍根を残してしまったこともあります。一方で，20世紀以降の世界では，そうした宗教間の対立を乗り越えるために様々な形の宗教間対話が重ねられてきました。現代ではさらに，キリスト教であれ，イスラム教であれ，仏教であれ，自分の宗教とは違う宗教の中味（神学）を，互いに深く学び合う必要性も叫ばれています。

6 CULTURAL NOTES

　ダライ・ラマは，チベット仏教の最上位のラマ（チベット語で「師」の意味）で，「大海」を意味するモンゴル語のダライをつけた称号です。チベット仏教では，輪廻転生が信じられており，現在のダライ・ラマ14世は，ダライ・ラマ13世の（もとをたどると観音菩薩の）生まれ変わりとされています。チベットでは，1959年に中国からの圧力に抗議した動乱が起こり，政府はインド北部のダラムサラに亡命しました。ダライ・ラマは，宗教の指導者であるとともに，チベット政府の元首の地位を兼ねています。

　ダライ・ラマ14世は非常に活動的で，世界各地を訪れ，イギリスのチャールズ皇太子やオバマ元アメリカ大統領をはじめ，多くの人々と親交があります。日本にも何度も訪れ，宗教の枠を超えた対話を行ったことでも知られています。

7 READING SECTION NOTES

l. 1.　Tibetan Buddhism　チベット仏教

l.20.　connectedness　つながり

l.29.　brotherhood　兄弟愛

8 LECTURE NOTES

l. 1.　Tenzin Gyatso　テンイン・ギャツォ，ダライ・ラマ 14 世の法名

l. 1.　His Holiness　聖下。ローマ教皇の尊称

l. 4.　install　任命する

l. 7.　adhere to　〜に忠実である

l.16.　pay homage to　〜に敬意を表する

l.19.　liberation　解放（運動）

9 SUMMARY SAMPLE

The theme of the Lecture is the Dalai Lama's respect for different religions and cultures.　He is the leader of Tibetan Buddhism who has had conversations with people of various backgrounds.　The Lecture says, in 1994, he was invited by a group of Christians to share his interpretation of certain passages of the Bible.　He referred to the Christian audience as "spiritual brothers and sisters."　The Reading Section says he talked about respecting all people as members of one family.

He met with civil rights leaders in Memphis in the United States.　He paid homage to the late Martin Luther King, Jr. The Dalai Lama spoke softly and expressed his appreciation for the civil rights movement.　He referred to Dr. King's famous *I Have a Dream* speech and spoke of his own dream of Tibetan liberation.　His charm is his ability to identify with others.

He also visited Hiroshima in 2010. He praised the Japanese people for their remarkable recovery after World War II. He said that the Japanese built a great nation after suffering so much during the war. He jokingly said that they should study English in order to be global. Of course, everyone knows that the Dalai laughs about his own poor English speaking ability.

1 READING SECTION

Read the following passage for 3 minutes.

Viktor Frankl was a Jewish Holocaust survivor who wrote a famous book about his survival of that terrible ordeal in Auschwitz, a Nazi concentration camp. The book is called *Man's Search for Meaning*. Frankl was trained as a psychiatrist, philosopher, and a scholar of religion. In the middle of his book, he included the following words: "I called to the Lord from my narrow prison and He answered me in the freedom of space."

5

These words are part of the Book of Psalms in the Bible (Psalm 118:5). Both Jews and Christians cherish the Psalms. The terms, "the Lord" and "He," with a capitalized "H," both refer to God. The writer of the psalm believes God, though invisible, is listening to human cries. There are two key expressions in the quotation that have obvious application to Frankl's war sufferings: *Prison* and *freedom of space*.

10

As Frankl describes Auschwitz, it was a *prison* which emphasized torture. The men were beaten, ill-fed, and poorly clothed. They were made to fight over small bits of bread. Frankl mentions that not all of the men resorted to fighting like animals among themselves. Some men shared their portions with weaker prisoners. Certainly, some human beings maintain their goodness even in hellish circumstances.

15

20

Getting out of any prison must be a happy experience. Frankl recalls the liberation by the Russian soldiers. He recalled that after liberation, he did indeed find himself in a wide open space. He fell to his knees on the grass and shed tears of joy for the *freedom of space.*

Recently, some critics have claimed that Viktor Frankl was treated more humanely than other Jewish prisoners. They claim that the Nazis gave him some privileges because of his high education. Even in such a case, a prison can never be a welcoming place.

25

2 LISTENING SECTION

Listen to a lecture on the topic you just read about.

3 QUESTION (SUMMARY)

Summarize the points made in the lecture, being sure to explain how the Reading Section deepens the understanding of the lecture passage (150 to 225 words). You have 20 minutes to plan and write your response.

4 LECTURE TRANSCRIPT

Dr. Viktor Frankl achieved international prominence for his work in psychiatric counselling and for his 1959 publication, *Man's Search for Meaning.* He was born in Vienna, Austria-Hungary in 1905. As a Jew, he was subjected to the discrimination and cruelty of the Nazis. He, his wife, his father, and other relatives were assigned to live in a ghetto in Czechoslovakia. Even though the Nazis claimed that this was a "model community" for middle-class Jews, it was obvious that Viktor Frankl's family had no choice in the matter of residence. In the ghetto, Frankl was allowed to practice psychiatry. He counselled new arrivals. Later, he focused his attention on preventing suicides among the depressed Jews.

5

10

In 1943, Frankl and his wife were transported to Auschwitz, Poland. They were separated. He was sent to the men's unit which housed over 2,000 prisoners. He would learn after the war that his wife died in a women's prison shortly before liberation in 1945. Unaware of his wife's fate, Frankl focused on the memory of her face. Having that vision gave him a pur- 15 pose for surviving. And, that is the premise of all of Dr. Frankl's work called logotherapy. Human beings can survive almost anything if they have a purpose. In his counselling of seriously depressed people in and out of concentration camps, Frankl encouraged people to find a purpose for continuing the struggles of life. It may be the thought of a lover, or some 20 important work that gives meaning to our lives. In the absence of a work or a lover, a person can even find meaning in preserving happy memories.

After the war, Frankl attained a Ph.D. in philosophy. He married a Roman Catholic woman who agreed with him in appreciating both faiths. *Man's Search for Meaning* continues to inspire many people. 25

5 BIBLE FOR GLOBAL LITERACY

"I called to the Lord from my narrow prison and He answered me in the freedom of space." （上記 **READING SECTION** 内の，ヴィクトール・E・フランクル『夜と霧』英語版にある言葉）
"Out of my distress I called on the LORD; the LORD answered me and set me in a broad place." (Psalm 118:5 [NRSV])

「苦難のはざまから主を呼び求めると　主は答えてわたしを解き放たれた。」（詩編118編5節）

　この言葉も旧約聖書『詩編』からの引用です。1章の **BIBLE FOR GLOBAL LITERACY** に記したように，『詩編』は古代イスラエル民族の信仰や祈りが詩（歌）という文学類型で記されている書です。万葉集に季節を詠んだ歌や恋の歌，挽歌などいろいろな歌が含まれるように，『詩編』にもいろいろな種類の詩があります。信仰の詩ですから，神への賛美や感謝を表した詩もあるのですが，実は『詩編』で一番多いのは「嘆きの祈り (lament)」に分類される詩なのです。
　詩編118編も，そんな「嘆きの祈り」の一つです。ここで言う「嘆き」は，単に悲嘆に暮れる

とか，厭世的になることではありません。『詩編』の「嘆き」は，人生の苦難に直面した者が，まさにその苦難の故に神に対して自らの思いを吐露するものです。つまりこれは，自分で自分を哀れむ自己憐憫ではなく，絶対者である神に自分の窮状を（祈りを通して）訴えるという信仰の表明なのです。

　苦しみに会ったとき，人間はその苦しみにどう向き合うかが問われます。苦しみを否定したり，そこから逃避したりしたい気持ちもあるでしょう。しかし，苦しいときは苦しいと訴えて良いこと，そしてその訴えを，自分よりも大きな存在である神にぶつけることを嘆きの詩編は示しています。ナチスの収容所にいたフランクルが上記の言葉を引用したことは，極限の苦しみの中にあっても心の内に自由を持つことができるという，人間の可能性と希望を示唆しているようです。

6 CULTURAL NOTES

　第2次世界大戦中にナチス・ドイツがユダヤ人などに対して組織的に行った大量虐殺（ホロコースト）では，想像を絶する数百万人ものユダヤ人が殺されました。収容所へ送られる前は，ゲットーと呼ばれるユダヤ人居住区域に住むことが強制されました。戦争の狂気の中でのことであっても，誰にも他の人の自由や命を奪う権利はありません。せめて今私たちができることは，戦争の現実を見つめ，二度と同じ過ちを繰り返さないようにすることではないかと思います。ヴィクトール・フランクルの『夜と霧』を読んでみましょう。

7 READING SECTION NOTES

l. 1. Holocaust　（特にナチスのユダヤ人に対する）大虐殺

l. 2. ordeal　恐ろしい体験

l. 4. psychiatrist　精神科医, psychiatric　精神医学の

l.15. Auschwitz　アウシュビッツ強制収容所

l.18. resort to 〜　〜することに訴える

l.20. hellish　地獄のような

l.22. liberation　釈放

l.23. fall to one's knees　ひざまづく

l.26. the Nazis　ナチ党

8 LECTURE NOTES

l. 1. achieve prominence　注目されるようになる

l. 3. subjected to 〜　〜を受ける

l. 5. ghetto　ユダヤ人街（強制居住区）

l.17. logotherapy　言語治療

l.19. concentration camp　強制収容所

9 SUMMARY SAMPLE

Viktor Frankl is famous for his book, *Man's Search for Meaning*, published in 1959. He tells of his experience in a concentration camp in World War II. As Jews, he, his wife, and father were transported to Auschwitz, Poland. He and his wife were separated at the camp. He did not know that his wife had died in the camp until after the war. His book focuses on his survival technique: focusing on something precious. For him, the image of his wife's face was his inspiration for continuing to struggle. Before he was sent to the camp, Frankl counseled many Jews who were depressed. He taught that people can survive almost anything if they focus on something good. He, himself, experienced horrors during imprisonment. The Reading Section gives some details of the prison experience: men were beaten, and they had to fight each other for a piece of bread. Thinking of his wife made him determined to live. His book explains his idea of logotherapy which encourages people to find a reason for their lives. After the war, Frankl married a Christian woman. They appreciated both Jewish and Christian faiths. Although he was already a psychiatrist, Frankl earned a Ph.D. in philosophy after the war. *Man's Search for Meaning is* still a popular book today.

1 READING SECTION

Read the following passage for 3 minutes.

Ted Turner is the founder of the CNN television network. Established in 1980, CNN was the first cable TV channel that ran news twenty-four hours. Turner is a billionaire and is known for his generosity; he has donated much of his fortune to the United Nations and to charities. 5

Turner's early life was not easy. As a teenager, he witnessed the poor health and suffering of his sister. Although his family background was Christian, Turner became bitter toward all religions. He concluded that there was no god. Turner thought a god would not allow such pain to afflict his sister and family. 10

Despite his negative thoughts about religions, he has helped many people with his money. He has even pledged a large portion of his fortune to be distributed to several charities after he dies. He may not be religious, but he demonstrates the idea that kind actions are more important than words. Once, he used the following to explain 15 his charitable giving: "It is better to give than to receive." These are the words of Jesus as quoted by Paul, a first century Christian teacher.

These words appear in the Bible story of Paul's farewell to his friends. He appreciated the hospitality shown to him, and he encouraged them to extend their hospitality to others, particularly the poor 20 people in their community. Always Paul was aware of the needs of underprivileged people. His teaching emphasized not focusing on getting "silver or gold." Rather, everyone should work hard to relieve the suffering of the poor. His idea is that we can achieve happiness by taking care of other people's needs. This idea continues to chal- 25 lenge all people today. We should all understand the need to share. The world is a better place when people focus on giving more than receiving.

2 LISTENING SECTION

Listen to a lecture on the topic you just read about.

3 QUESTION (SUMMARY)

Summarize the points made in the lecture, being sure to explain how the Reading Section deepens the understanding of the lecture passage (150 to 225 words). You have 20 minutes to plan and write your response.

4 LECTURE TRANSCRIPT

When Ted Turner was born in Cincinnati, Ohio in 1938, there were very few television sets in American homes. Now, even the poorest homes have T.V. sets. Many of them are tuned in to CNN, or Cable News Network, which Turner created in the early 1980s. Because of his organization, peo- ple have immediate access to news about the latest medical discoveries, the 5 achievements in the arts, religious events, and of course, the conflicts be- tween nations.

Turner is a genius in the world of communication technology. But maybe he is not so adept at personal communication. He is known for his gruff manner. He is capable of saying shocking things, especially about religion. 10

At different times he has announced himself an atheist and an agnostic. An atheist is one who does not believe in God, and an agnostic is a person who cannot say if God exists or not. He has publicly insulted Christians, saying, "Christianity is for losers."

However, Turner should not be dismissed as a mean man. Despite his words, he has spent a considerable portion of his fortune on causes which benefit many people, Christians included. In fact, he has financed the United Nations Conference on World Religion in the year 2000. Additionally, he regularly gives money to the Atlanta Ballet and the Red Cross. He also sponsors various organizations that champion women's rights. He encourages young African American artists.

One of the things few people know about him is that he is the second largest individual landowner in the United States. On his numerous ranches, he protects 51,000 buffalo. They were once near extinction, but Turner has caused an increase in their numbers. Clearly, he is a man whose good works benefit the planet. Perhaps he reminds us all that we should focus more on people's good works rather than on their gruff manner.

5 BIBLE FOR GLOBAL LITERACY

"In everything I did, I showed you that by this kind of hard work we must help the weak, remembering the words the Lord Jesus himself said: 'It is more blessed to give than to receive.'" (**Acts 20:35 [NIV]**)

「あなたがたもこのように働いて弱い者を助けるように，また，主イエス御自身が『受けるよりは与える方が幸いである』と言われた言葉を思い出すようにと，わたしはいつも身をもって示してきました。」（使徒言行録20章35節）

　『使徒言行録』には，キリストが去った後に弟子達がキリストの教えを広めていく様子が描かれています。この際に，中心的な役割を果たした人物としてこの書に描かれているのがパウロという人物です。上記の言葉は，このパウロがエフェソ（17章の **BIBLE FOR GLOBAL LITERACY**

参照）の教会指導者に語った言葉の一部であり，『　』内はイエス・キリストの言葉の引用です。

　この言葉は，イエスが語った教えに多い「逆説の妙」を示した言葉になっています。誰しも，お金や物を他者から「受け取ること」や「もらうこと」は喜ばしいと思うものです。しかしイエスは，逆に他者に「与えること」の方が真の幸いではないかと問いかけているのです。

　アメリカ合衆国では寄付の文化が根付いていると言われ，信じられない程の多額の寄付金があったとニュースで取り上げられることがあります。そうしたことの背景にこの聖書の言葉があるのかもしれません。

6 CULTURAL NOTES

　CNN は，ワーナーメディアの一部門であるワーナー・メディア・ニュース・スポーツが所有するアメリカのケーブルテレビおよび衛星テレビ向けのニュースチャンネルです。1980 年にテッド・ターナーによって世界初の 24 時間放送するニュース専門のチャンネルとして設立されました。本社はジョージア州アトランタで，国際放送は，200 以上の国と地域で視聴可能です。世界の特定の地域や言語に向けたローカルメディアを立ち上げる事にも積極的で，アジアの多くのホテルでは，CNN Asia を視聴することができます。

7 READING SECTION NOTES

l.10.　afflict　（肉体的または精神的に）苦しめる

l.12.　pledge　誓約する

l.16.　charitable giving　慈善事業への寄付

l.22.　underprivileged people　恵まれない人々

8 LECTURE NOTES

l. 9.　adept　熟達した。〜が上手である。

l. 9.　gruff manner　ぶっきらぼうな態度

l.11.　atheist　無神論者

l.11.　agnostic　不可知論者（神様の存在を証明することは不可能であるという見解を持った人）

l.23.　ranch　大牧場

9 SUMMARY SAMPLE

Ted Turner was born in the 1930s when there were not so many television sets in American homes. However, he created Cable News Network; many people are familiar with his achievement. He is a genius in technology, but some people are not convinced of his communication skills. He speaks in a rough manner, and he has insulted many people. He seems bitter toward Christianity. The Reading Section says that he stopped being a Christian when he was a teenager. His sister became sick and suffered very much. That caused Turner to abandon his faith. However, he made millions of dollars, and he contributes much to charity; sometimes Christians benefit from his donations. He even sponsored the United Nations Conference on World Religion. The Reading Section also says that he plans for his charities to continue after he dies. The Lecture says that people should probably be judged more for their good works than they are judged for the things they say.

Chapter 24 / *Eddie Redmayne*

1 READING SECTION

Read the following passage for 3 minutes.

Eddie Redmayne, the Academy Award-winning actor, attended the funeral for his good friend, Stephen Hawking at St. Mary's Church in London in March 2018. Although there was a 40-year difference in their ages, the two had become great friends during the filming of *The Theory of Everything*. Redmayne portrayed Hawking, a famous physicist who suffered from ALS, a terrible disease which damaged his body. Hawking had announced that he did not believe in God, but his family insisted on having a Christian funeral. They asked Eddie Redmayne to read a Bible passage at the service. He read Ecclesiastes 3:1-11. The theme is *appropriateness*, knowing when it is right to do certain things. The passage is famous and has been set to music by different composers. It is not a forceful statement on major Christian teachings. Instead it shows an understanding of when certain human behaviors are acceptable. Among the famous words are:

There is a time for everything,
and a season for every activity under heaven.
A time to be born and a time to die,
A time to plant and a time to uproot ...
A time to weep and a time to laugh ...

Ecclesiastes 3:1-11 suggests that the intelligent person recognizes which reactions are needed in certain situations. It begins with a reference to planting and harvesting. These are activities which require an understanding of what must be done in each season. Similarly, there are certain necessary responses in human interactions. The passage covers a wide range of human responses to situations. Human beings who are socially mature understand the appropriate times for laughter, crying, and silence.

As a serious scientist who lectured on physics, Hawking was aware of the importance of timing. He knew that physics requires intense concentration. It is necessary to include some moments of relaxation in the midst of study. He interspersed humor in his presentations. Even in his classroom there was "a time to laugh." Ecclesiastes was the appropriate reading for the funeral of such an intelligent scientist as Stephen Hawking.

2 LISTENING SECTION

Listen to a lecture on the topic you just read about.

3 QUESTION (SUMMARY)

Summarize the points made in the lecture, being sure to explain how the Reading Section deepens the understanding of the lecture passage (150 to 225 words). You have 20 minutes to plan and write your response.

4 LECTURE TRANSCRIPT

Eddie Redmayne is one of the most popular international actors. He is an Academy Award winner. He was born in London in 1982. Growing up in the 1980s and 1990s, Redmayne enjoyed the privileges of middle-class life.

As a child, he attended an acting school where he developed his skills in singing and performance. He graduated in 2003 from Trinity College, in Cambridge, UK. Queen Elizabeth II of England recognized Redmayne's talents. In 2015, she presented him with the prestigious Order of the British Empire (O.B.E.).

His versatility includes modeling for the Burberry clothing brand, acting in Shakespearean dramas on stage, and portraying very complex real-life characters in movies. One of the complex characters he has portrayed is Stephen Hawking, the British scholar of physics. Redmayne's 2014 Academy Award was for portraying him in the film, *The Theory of Everything*. Hawking was stricken with a serious disease when he was only 21 years old. Eventually, Hawking became wheelchair bound. His body was contorted, and he required a special computer in order to speak. In the process of preparing for the role, Redmayne spent much time with Hawking, taking note of his mannerisms and personality.

Often Redmayne is featured in roles which capitalize on his good looks. However, for his portrayal of the real-life genius, he had to present himself as an aging man with a disability. Redmayne convincingly portrayed Hawking's deteriorating health. Importantly, Redmayne was able to capture two things in the film: Hawking's undiminished intelligence and his charm appeal.

In the process of spending time with Hawking, Redmayne achieved something greater than his numerous acting awards. He developed a deep bond with Stephen Hawking. When Redmayne received the Academy Award, Hawking sent him a congratulatory note. Four years later, Hawking died. Redmayne was asked to speak at the funeral. He said: "We have lost a truly beautiful mind, an astonishing scientist and the funniest man I have ever had the pleasure to meet."

5 BIBLE FOR GLOBAL LITERACY

"There is a time for everything, and a season for every activity under the heavens: a time to be born and a time to die, a time to plant and a time to uproot, ... a time to weep and a time to laugh, ... He has made everything beautiful in its time. He has also set eternity in the human heart ..." (Ecclesiastes 3:1-2, 4, 11 [NIV])

「何事にも時があり　天の下の出来事にはすべて定められた時がある。生まれる時，死ぬ時　植える時，植えたものを抜く時…泣く時，笑う時…神はすべてを時宜にかなうように造り，また，永遠を思う心を人に与えられる。…」（コヘレトの言葉 3 章 1 節-2 節，4 節，11 節）

　「コヘレトの言葉」は聖書の中でも異色の書と言えます。まず，この書の著者が誰か明確にわかっていません。記したのは「コヘレト」であると冒頭部分に書かれてあるのですが，「コヘレト」とはヘブライ語で「（語るために）集会を招集する人」を意味する言葉にすぎず，それが具体的に誰を指すのかは不明です。英語の書名である "Ecclesiastes" は，「コヘレト」のギリシア語訳が元になっているため，日本語の書名と全く違った言葉になっています。

　この書はまた，ヘブライ語聖書（旧約聖書）の一部でありながらギリシア思想の影響が見受けられる点でも異色と言えます。その一つの例が，ここに掲げられた「時」や「永遠」に関する言葉です。ギリシア語には「客観的な時間，例えば時計でみる時間」を表す「クロノス」と，「主観的な時間，機会」を表す「カイロス」という二つの「時」概念があります。もちろんこの二つの概念は交錯することもあるのですが，あえて違いを意識してみることもできます。例えば，"What time is it?" という問いは，「いま何時ですか」とも訳せますが，「カイロス」的に「いまはどんな時・時代か」，あるいは「いまは何をすべき時か」という問いとも解釈できます。そうしてみると，人がより意識すべきは「カイロス」ではないでしょうか。キリスト教の影響が見られる文学やスピーチの中では，上記の言葉を通して「時・カイロス」を「神の時」として見据える視点がしばしば見受けられます。

6 CULTURAL NOTES

　スティーヴン・ホーキング博士は，宇宙の始まり「ビッグバン」がどのように起こったのか，あらゆる物質を飲み込んでしまう「ブラックホール」の内部はどうなっているのかなどについて，数式と理論で解明しようとした宇宙物理学者です。大学生の時に発症した，全身の筋肉が徐々に動かなくなる筋委縮性側索硬化症（ALS）と闘い続けてきた「車いすの天才科学者」として知られています。この病気は通常 5 年程度が寿命と言われますが，ホーキング博士については病気の進行が緩慢で，50 年以上この分野の常識を覆す様々な理論を発表しました。晩年は，ALS のため声を失いましたが，コンピュータソフトウェア会社として有名な intel のチームが，わずかに動く頬の筋肉と連動させて声を合成することに成功し，その装置を使ってコミュニケーションをしていました。

　映画『博士と彼女のセオリー』（2014 年）では，エディ・レッドメインがホーキング博士を演じ，アカデミー賞主演男優賞をはじめとする数々の賞を総なめにしました。エディ・レッドメインは，映画『ハリー・ポッター』シリーズのスピンオフである『ファンタスティック・ビースト』シリーズ（2016 年〜）で，主役の魔法動物学者ニュート・スキャマンダーを演じています。現代イギリスを代表する俳優です。

7 READING SECTION NOTES

l. 6.　ALS (amyotrophic lateral sclerosis)　筋委縮性索硬化症

l.10.　appropriateness　適切性

l.12.　forceful　力強い

l.23.　harvest　収穫する

l.32.　intersperse　散りばめる

8 LECTURE NOTES

l. 3.　the privileges　特権・恩恵

l. 7.　prestigious　名誉ある

l. 7.　Order of the British Empire (OBE)　大英国勲位

l. 9.　versatility　多様な能力

l.15.　contorted　ねじ曲がった

l.18.　mannerism　くせ

l.21.　disability　障害

l.21.　convincingly　もっともらしく

l.22.　deteriorating　悪化している

l.23.　undiminished　衰えていない

9 SUMMARY SAMPLE

Eddie Redmayne is a famous British actor. He grew up in a middle-class family in London. He was privileged to attend a special school which taught acting, singing, and performance. Eventually he graduated from Trinity College of Cambridge University. Over the years, he has acted on the stage and in movies. In 2014, he received the Academy Award for portraying the life of Stephen Hawking, the famous British physicist. Queen Elizabeth II gave Redmayne a prize, the Order of the British Empire (O.B.E.).

During the course of the filming, Redmayne researched Hawking's life and studied his mannerisms and personality. The two of them formed a deep friendship. The Reading Section notes that there was 40-year age difference between the two men. Despite that difference they expressed their deep feelings for each other. When Redmayne got the Academy Award, Hawking sent a note of congratulations. A few years later, Hawking died. Redmayne spoke at the funeral. He said that Hawking was the funniest man he had ever met. The Reading Section says that Redmayne chose a Bible passage which says that there is a time to laugh. That sentence seems to reflect on their happy friendship.

1 READING SECTION

Read the following passage for 3 minutes.

Wangari Maathai, the first African woman to win the Nobel Prize (2004), delivered the main speech at the Third Annual Nelson Mandela Lecture in Johannesburg, South Africa on July 19, 2005. Her speech honored the many charities which focused on the poor people in many African countries. She saluted Bob Geldof and Bono for raising money at their musical events. But her vision was that poor Africans would one day be able to sustain themselves. A key expression she used to explain her vision was, "Rise up and walk." The phrase was actually a direct quotation from Acts 3:6 in the Bible. [5]

In fact, Maathai went on to explain the whole story of the Bible in which the phrase was spoken. The story begins with two students of Jesus walking to the temple. It was 3:00 o'clock in the afternoon. At that moment, a crippled man was being carried near the front door of the temple. This was his daily routine; friends would leave him there to beg. When he saw Peter and John, two students of Jesus, he asked them for money. In the manner of beggars, he held his head down, not making eye contact. However, Peter surprised the handicapped man. He asked the man to look directly at him. Then Peter announced that he didn't have "silver or gold," but he would give him what he had. Then Peter said the famous words, "Rise up and walk." He extended his hand to lift the man up. Miraculously, the man could stand on his own. More than that, he could jump up joyously. [10] [15] [20]

Happy about his healing, the poor man walked into the temple with Peter and John.

Referring to this story in the Bible, Wangari Maathai was asking rich nations to provide technical training and schools to the poor people of African countries. Educated and employed people can feel good about themselves and proceed to help others.

25

2 LISTENING SECTION

Listen to a lecture on the topic you just read about.

3 QUESTION (SUMMARY)

Summarize the points made in the lecture, being sure to explain how the Reading Section deepens the understanding of the lecture passage (150 to 225 words). You have 20 minutes to plan and write your response.

4 LECTURE TRANSCRIPT

Sometimes called "Mamma Miti," which means "Mother of Trees" in Swahili, Dr. Wangari Maathai was a woman of great education. She was born in Kenya in 1940, and during her 71 years of life, she achieved fame as an environmental and political activist. When she visited Japan in 2005, she delighted audiences with her brightly colored African garb, her smile, and her newly-learned Japanese word, *Mottainai*.

5

The year before her arrival in Japan, Maathai had received the Nobel Prize for Peace. She earned many university degrees culminating in the Ph.D. in Veterinary Anatomy, a study of animals, particularly cows. She traveled around the world encouraging people to plant trees. With her head covered in a traditional scarf, and with seedlings and saplings in her hands, she did

10

not fit the image most people had of a university professor. In fact, she was associated with research at the University of Giessen in Germany and with the University of Nairobi. She was happy when she inserted young plants in the rich soil around the world.

15

Maathai was interested in more than trees and cows. While teaching at the University of Nairobi in 1977, she demanded that women employees be given equal benefits and salaries to men. She even helped organize a union. Her focus on ecology and human rights caused her husband to divorce her. He declared that he was "unable to control her." Further, her husband accused her of having an affair with a member of the Kenyan Parliament. Although she denied it, she was sentenced to six months in jail. Lawyers got her out of jail in three days. She died in 2011. She was accorded a formal state funeral and praised by the President of Kenya—the same president who, in 2008, ordered her and fellow protesters to be teargassed for opposing his government policies.

20

25

5 BIBLE FOR GLOBAL LITERACY

"... rise up and walk." (Acts 3:6 [KJV])

「ペトロとヨハネが，午後三時の祈りの時に神殿に上って行った。すると，生まれながら足の不自由な男が運ばれて来た。神殿の境内に入る人に施しを乞うため，毎日『美しい門』という神殿の門のそばに置いてもらっていたのである。… その男が，何かもらえると思って二人を見つめていると，ペトロは言った。『わたしには金や銀はないが，持っているものをあげよう。ナザレの人イエス・キリストの名によって**立ち上がり，歩きなさい**。』そして，右手を取って彼を立ち上がらせた。すると，たちまち，その男は足やくるぶしがしっかりして，躍り上がって立ち，歩きだした。…」（使徒言行録 3 章 1 節-2 節，5 節-8 節）

　ワンガリ・マータイが用いた聖書の表現（上記英語部分）は，新約聖書『使徒言行録』に記されている，あるエピソードに出てくる言葉です。日本語聖書部分が，この話のあらましです。
　ここに登場するのは，イエスの弟子であったペトロとヨハネ，そして金銭の施しを求める足の不自由な男性です。このときペトロは「わたしには金や銀はないが，持っているものをあげよう」と

言い，この男性の足は奇跡的に癒されます。つまり，この男性は少しばかりの金銭以上のものを手にしたのです。このエピソードが示唆しているのは，「魚を与えるのではなく，魚の釣り方を教えよ」との格言にも共通する考え方と言えるかもしれません。

　ちなみに，聖書に登場する人物の名前はカタカナで表記され，日本語としては耳慣れない名前ばかりかもしれません。しかし，こうした名前を英語に直すと，実は西洋社会で今も広く用いられている名前であることがわかります。たとえば，ペトロは英語で Peter，ヨハネは John，『使徒言行録』後半の中心人物であるパウロは Paul なのです。こうしたところにも，西洋社会の歴史において聖書が深く浸透していることが見てとれます。

6　CULTURAL NOTES

　ケニア出身の環境保護活動家，ワンガリ・マータイさんは，「グリーンベルト運動」で植林活動を行い，アフリカの持続可能な開発の推進に取り組みました。

　2005 年に環境問題（地球温暖化）に関する会議に出席するために来日した際，マータイさんは，環境問題に対処する 3R として知られる，Reduce（削減），Reuse（再利用），Recycle（リサイクル）にあたる概念は日本にあるかを問いました。「もったいない」という考え方を知ると，この概念には，3R の他に，もう一つの R である Respect（使ったり食べたりするもの，ひいてはそれを作った人や自然への感謝・尊敬の念）が含まれていると考えました。彼女の来日後，「もったいない」キャンペーンが行われ，再利用できる風呂敷の価値が見直されたり，若い世代への働きかけで，子

どもたちによるフリーマーケットなどが開催されたりしました。

　「もったいない」という言葉と概念は，国外にも広まりました。インドネシアでは「もったいないダンス」が，ベトナムでは「もったいない祭」があるそうです（毎日新聞，2018年7月）。

7 READING SECTION NOTES

l. 5.　salute　賞賛する

l. 7.　sustain oneself　自活する

l.13.　crippled　手足の不自由な

l.15.　beg　施しを乞う

l.16.　beggar　乞食

l.23.　healing　治療

8 LECTURE NOTES

l. 3.　achieve fame　有名になる

l. 5.　garb　服装

l. 8.　culminate　（結果的に）～になる

l. 9.　Veterinary Anatomy　獣医解剖学

l.11.　seedling　種，苗木,

l.11.　sapling　苗木

l.23.　accord someone a state funeral　～を国葬にする

l.25.　protester　抗議（行動を）する人

l.25.　tear-gas　催涙ガスを浴びせる

9 SUMMARY SAMPLE

Wangari Maathai, Nobel Peace Prize winner in 2004, was born in Kenya. She had many university degrees. She traveled around the world. She was interested in people and in nature. She visited Japan in 2005. She encouraged tree-planting around the world. According to the Reading Section, she visited South Africa and participated in an event honoring Bob Geldof and Bono, two musicians who raised money for poor Africans. While in Nairobi, she helped organize a union. She wanted women and men to have equal salaries. Although she was busy supporting ecology as well as human rights, her husband was not pleased. He divorced her. He claimed that she was having an affair with another man. Maathai denied it. Nevertheless, she was sentenced to jail for six months. Despite her personal problems, she brought honor to her country. As the Reading Section says, Wangari Maathai wanted rich nations to provide technical training schools for poor Africans. Her Nobel Prize, and her constant efforts to protect the environment and people caused the government to give her a formal state funeral.

1 READING SECTION

Read the following passage for 3 minutes.

In 2011, when he was a few weeks away from his 100th birthday, Dr. Shigeaki Hinohara spoke at International Christian University in Tokyo. Although he had distinguished himself in the medical field, Dr. Hinohara's focus in that speech was on the importance of studying the arts. He talked about his illness in childhood. He learned to play the piano, and even at 100 years old he could still play classical music. Also, as a child, he learned to be patient in his illness. He was half joking to the University audience when he said, "You all should become sick, though not enough to die." Hinohara was suggesting that if we are patient in our suffering, we will learn many things. Suffering sickness at such an early age taught him to be a sensitive doctor when he got older. He understood pain, and he devoted his long life to relieving people of their pain. He quoted the Bible: "Blessed is the one who perseveres under trial because, having stood the test, that person will receive the crown of life that the Lord has promised to those who love him."

In 1970, Hinohara was on board Japan Airlines Flight 351 when it was hijacked by terrorists. The plane was forced to land near Seoul, Korea. Passengers were handcuffed and given very little food. Hinohara comforted passengers as much as he could. At the end of three days, the terrible experience ended.

The Bible passage, James 1:12, does not mean that if we are patient we will escape hard times and death. Everyone eventually dies. The message of the Bible is that if we are patient, we will realize some good result. In those two traumas, the experience of childhood illness, and the experience of being a hostage, Dr. Hinohara developed a deepened sensitivity to people who are troubled.

25

2 LISTENING SECTION

Listen to a lecture on the topic you just read about.

3 QUESTION (SUMMARY)

Summarize the points made in the lecture, being sure to explain how the Reading Section deepens the understanding of the lecture passage (150 to 125 words). You have 20 minutes to plan and write your response.

4 LECTURE TRANSCRIPT

Dr. Shigeaki Hinohara was remarkable for many reasons, not just the fact that he lived to be 105 years old. He was born in Yamaguchi Prefecture in 1911. He was not a healthy child, and he spent many days sick in bed. His mother encouraged him to take advantage of the days he could not go outside; she recommended that he learn to play the piano.

5

When his mother, herself, became very ill, he observed her doctor's dedicated care. It was then he decided that he would one day become a medical doctor. He once said that his mother's illness, as well as his own, gave him insight into the needs of patients. Eventually, he graduated from Kyoto University School of Medicine. He further studied at Emory University in the United States. When he returned to Japan, he was appointed

10

as the Chief of Internal Medicine at St. Luke's International Hospital in Tokyo. Among the several universities which have honored him are: Kyoto Imperial University, Thomas Jefferson University in America, and McMaster University in Canada.

Throughout World War II, Hinohara cared for the sick and injured in the firebombing of Tokyo. In more modern times, he advised hospitals on the care of the injured in the sarin attack on Tokyo subways in 1995. Later, he promoted annual medical checkups, saving many lives.

Even though he achieved fame as a talented physician, Dr. Hinohara continued his interest in music. At the age of 88 he composed a musical for children, even acting in the performance. He was one of the first people to consider the good effect soothing music has on the healing of sick people. He served as Honorary President of the Japan Music Therapy Association. He wrote the Greetings to the meeting of music therapists for their conference which was held in Tsukuba, Japan. He died a contented man in 2017.

5 BIBLE FOR GLOBAL LITERACY

"Blessed is the one who perseveres under trial because, having stood the test, that person will receive the crown of life that the Lord has promised to those who love him." (James 1:12 [NIV])

「試練を耐え忍ぶ人は幸いです。その人は適格者と認められ，神を愛する人々に約束された命の冠をいただくからです。」（ヤコブの手紙 1 章 12 節）

　新約聖書には，『福音書』，『使徒言行録』に続いて，初期のキリスト教指導者が仲間のキリスト教徒に書き送った多くの手紙が収録されています。上記はその一つで，イエス・キリストの弟であり，エルサレム教会の指導者でもあったヤコブが記したとされる手紙になります。
　苦しいことがあったとき，それを行き詰まりの状態ととらえるのではなく，「その苦しみを味わったことによってのみ開かれる将来に向けての必要な過程」ととらえることもできます。聖書では，そのような過程は「試練」とも表現されます。そして，苦しみや試練に出会ったときに必要なのは忍耐・粘り強さ（perseverance）であるとヤコブは記しています。「命の冠」とは，とりわけ信仰の

故に迫害を受けた者が天で神から与えられるとされるものの象徴であり，苦しみは究極的に苦しみで終わらないことを示唆しています。

　個人の手のひらにあるスマホ（スマートフォン）によって膨大な情報が瞬時に手に入る現代では，苦しみの解決策も容易なはずである，それが手に入らないのは単に情報が足りないからであると錯覚しがちかもしれません。しかし，例えば病気の理由として細菌やウイルスがあることを知らなかった古代の人々は，苦しみを試練ととらえ，忍耐を重んじました。科学を修めた医師である日野原さんが，一方でこうした古代の書物である聖書の言葉から多くを学んでいたことは，私たちに何を教えているのでしょうか。

6 CULTURAL NOTES

　日野原重明氏が，名誉会長を務めた日本音楽療法学会によると，音楽療法は音楽を用いたセラピーで，「音楽のもつ生理的，心理的，社会的働きを用いて，心身の障害の回復，機能の維持改善，生活の質の向上，行動の変容などに向けて，音楽を意図的，計画的に使用すること」と定義されています。単にうたを歌ったり，音楽を聴いたりするといったこととは違い，音楽療法士が個々のニーズに合わせて音楽を提供し，成果を分析しながら行う支援の方法であるとされています。音楽療法を受けた人と受けなかった人の比較で，受けた人の方が寿命が長かったという報告や，認知症高齢者領域で，不安と不穏そして敵意の軽減が報告されているということです。(https://www.jmta.jp/about/outline.html)

7 READING SECTION NOTES

l. 3.   distinguish oneself　卓越する

l.13.   relieve A of B　A から B を取り除く

l.14.   persevere　耐える

l.14.   trial　試練

l.15.   test　試練，苦難

l.19.   handcuff　手錠をかける

l.25.   trauma　心の傷，トラウマ

l.27.   sensitivity　気配り

8 LECTURE NOTES

l. 4.   take advantage of　～を活用する

l. 9.   give someone insight into　～に～という洞察力を与える

l.16.   the firebombing of Tokyo　東京大空襲

l.18.   sarin　サリン（毒ガス）

l.23.   soothing music　癒し系の音楽

l.25.   music therapist　音楽療法士

l.26.   contented　満足そうな

9 SUMMARY SAMPLE

Dr. Shigeaki Hinohara knew about suffering. Although he lived to be 105 years old, he was sickly in his childhood. His mother encouraged him to play the piano when he was child. She thought it would give him some relief during the days of being confined to the house. She, herself, became ill. When young Hinohara observed a doctor's good care of her, he was determined to grow up and become a physician. His interest in music persisted throughout his life. The Reading Section says that he gave a speech at International Christian University, celebrating his 100th birthday. He stressed the importance of the arts. He believed that music could help in healing. In fact, he served as Honorary President of the Japan Music Therapy Association. He composed a musical for children when he was 88. He even acted in the musical. He was always interested in bringing comfort to people. The Reading Section says that he was aboard a hijacked airplane. During the days of that episode, he comforted distraught passengers. Both the Reading Section and the Lecture describe a man who was eager to comfort others.

1 **READING SECTION**

Read the following passage for 3 minutes.

Thabo Mbeki, President of South Africa from 1999 to 2008, delivered a speech in which he quoted Proverbs 3:27-28: "Do not withhold good from those who deserve it, when it is within your power to act. Do not say to your neighbor, 'Come back later; I'll give it tomorrow.'" 5

He was speaking to a large audience comprised of African and European dignitaries. His education and cultured background were in evidence as he quoted Shakespeare and other Western writers. In addition to quoting the Bible and Shakespeare, Mbeki also quoted a traditional African concept, *Ubuntu*. He demonstrated how the Bible 10 and the African saying taught the same thing: human beings should be eager to offer immediate relief to someone who is suffering. Of course, he was applying that concept to some sympathetic whites who had said, "We agree blacks should be liberated, but they should be patient. Societies change slowly." 15

As a passionate freedom fighter who had become South Africa's second black president, Mbeki did not believe in being patient with suffering. He quoted several passages of world literature that taught immediate action against evil. Mbeki placed the African term, *Ubuntu*, on equal footing with Proverbs 3:27-28. He was eager to 20 demonstrate that the great ideas were universal. They were not limited to Western books. Africa, too, had profound and beautiful concepts.

Mbeki's speech was, itself, a literary masterpiece. But as some critics have noted, his cultured background and middle-class lifestyle made it difficult for him to identify with the people who suffered most in his society. He was focused on improving the image of the country. He secured the 2010 FIFA games, and he improved schools. However, the most destitute people still suffered from poor health, poor housing, and poor education. Some people say that Mbeki's legacy would be even greater if he had applied Proverbs 3:27–28 to the most severe cases of suffering.

25

30

2 LISTENING SECTION

Listen to a lecture on the topic you just read about.

3 QUESTION (SUMMARY)

Summarize the points made in the lecture, being sure to explain how the Reading Section deepens the understanding of the lecture passage (150 to 225 words). You have 20 minutes to plan and write your response.

4 LECTURE TRANSCRIPT

Thabo Mbeki, only the second black President of South Africa, was born in Cape Province, 1942. Both of his parents were teachers. Two portraits were on the wall of their home: one of Karl Marx (German philosopher), and one of Mahatma Gandhi (religious leader and thinker). Education and art were important to him. As a young man, Mbeki developed a deep

5

appreciation for poetry and literature. He was fond of reading the dramas of Shakespeare. He and his friends frequented bars where they listened to jazz and blues music.

In the 1960's the black people of South Africa protested against the policy of *Apartheid,* which restricted their freedoms. Mbeki became an activist. He and several friends disguised themselves as football players and boarded a series of airplanes until they arrived in London, UK. While there, Mbeki organized events to make British people aware of the suffering of South Africans. In addition to his political activities, Mbeki earned a degree in economics from the University of Sussex. He returned to Africa in 1971, quickly becoming an important figure. He was imprisoned several different times for his political activities, but in 1994, Mbeki became deputy President of South Africa. Finally, he became President in 1997.

During his two terms as President, Mbeki was criticized for not making health care for AIDS patients a government priority. He insisted that the government should focus on economic improvement. It is generally agreed that he was responsible for a big growth of the South African middle class. The lower classes, however, did not see a major change in their lives. His emphasis on improving the image of South Africa led him to successfully host the 2010 FIFA World Cup. In short, Thabo Mbeki was a controversial leader. He supported the middle class; he was insufficiently attentive to the poorer people of society.

5 BIBLE FOR GLOBAL LITERACY

"Do not withhold good from those to whom it is due, when it is in your power to act. Do not say to your neighbor, 'Come back tomorrow and I'll give it to you'— when you already have it with you." (Proverbs 3:27-28 [NIV])

「施すべき相手に善行を拒むな　あなたの手にその力があるなら。出直してくれ，明日あげよう，と友に言うな　あなたが今持っているなら。」（箴言3章27節-28節）

　この言葉も，旧約聖書の格言集である「箴言」にある言葉です。箴言に含まれる言葉の多くは，必ずしも時間をかけて深く考える必要がある言葉ではありません。むしろ，言葉の短さも手伝って，単刀直入に行動の変化を求めるのが箴言の特徴と言えます。

　聖書には，忍耐すべき時，待つべき時が人間にはあると記されている箇所があります。この箴言の言葉は逆に，待っていてはいけない時，いますぐに行動すべき時もあると教えています。

　善行を拒むとまではいかなくても，善行を躊躇してしまうことは誰にでもあるでしょう。例えば，電車の中で誰かに席を譲ろうとして断られた体験があれば，再び席を譲る機会が訪れたときに思わず迷ってしまうかもしれません。上記の言葉は，豊かな国による開発途上国への援助に留まらず，一人一人ができることを，すみやかに行動に移すように促しています。

6 CULTURAL NOTES

　アパルトヘイトは，アフリカーンス語で「分離・隔離」を意味する語で，南アフリカ共和国における，白人と非白人の人種隔離政策を指します。1948 年に法制度として確立され，1994 年に全人種が参加する総選挙でネルソン・マンデラが初の黒人大統領に就任するまで続きました。マンデラ氏は民族和解・協調を呼びかけ，アパルトヘイト体制下での白人・黒人との対立や格差の是正，黒人間の対立の解消，経済制裁による経済不況からの回復に努めました。

　本章で扱った 2 代目大統領のムベキ政権下では黒人経済力増強政策がとられ，各企業に一定数の黒人登用を義務づけました。これにより黒人の中流層が勃興する一方で，アパルトヘイト時代に不十分な教育しか受けることのできなかった大多数の黒人は，この恩恵を受けることができず，貧富の差は拡大したと言われています。アパルトヘイトという人種差別政策は，南アフリカ共和国に長く暗い影を落としていると言わざるを得ません。

7 READING SECTION NOTES

l. 2.　withhold　差し控える

l. 7.　dignitary　（政府などの）要人

l. 7.　in evidence　はっきり見えて

l.14.　liberate　（社会的に）権利を与える

l.29.　destitute　極貧の

8 LECTURE NOTES

l.10.　apartheid　アパルトヘイト（南アフリカ共和国の人種隔離政策）

l.10.　activist　（政治的な改革を目指す）活動家

l.11.　disguise oneself as A　A の姿に変装する

l.16.　imprison　投獄する

9 SUMMARY SAMPLE

Thabo Mbeki was the second black president of South Africa. He came from an educated family. He was knowledgeable about Shakespeare and other Western writers. The Lecture states that as a young man he went to bars with friends and listened to American jazz and blues music. In the 1960s, Mbeki went to London and protested against the South African system of *Apartheid*. He wanted the world to know that black people did not have equality. He graduated with a degree in Economics from a British university. He returned to his country and eventually became president. Under his leadership, there were improvements in education and economics, but unfortunately, the poorest people did not benefit so much. The Reading Section mentions his impressive speech to an international audience. He talked about the connection between a Bible passage and an African concept. Both of these ideas teach giving immediate relief to suffering people. However, he is accused of not sufficiently attending to people suffering from AIDS and other severe problems. Rather, he focused on the country's image. For example, he promoted the 2010 FIFA World Cup in the country. In both the Lecture and the Reading Section, it mentions that poor people did not benefit from his leadership.

Chapter 28 / *David Suchet*

Read the following passage for 3 minutes.

In one of the most amazing feats of public performance, David Suchet read the entire Gospel of Mark at London's St. Paul's Cathedral in 2017. Of course, he is the distinguished actor who has won awards for portraying Detective Hercule Poirot on television, and *Macbeth* on stage. Nevertheless, it is remarkable that he held his audience spellbound as they listened to him read. The performance is easily accessible on YouTube. One person said, "I can hardly sit still for two hours. But it is wonderful that David Suchet could read so beautifully for two hours, never coughing or getting hoarse." The priest introduced Suchet's reading, saying that there were people standing around the block waiting to get inside the church. He joked that maybe those people misunderstood and thought that Beyonce' (the popular, sexy singer) was performing. But actually, David Suchet's talent is attractive enough to have drawn such huge crowds. He read the words spoken by Jesus: "... Come with me by yourselves to a quiet place and get some rest" (Mark 6:31).

The passage comes from the story about the popularity of Jesus as teacher. People crowded around him constantly. At that point in their lives, Jesus and his students attracted many followers. The Bible says that "So many people were coming and going (from their meetings) that Jesus and his friends did not have a chance to eat." To gain a little quiet time for themselves, Jesus invited his small group to a quiet place. Certainly, it is necessary for popular teachers, public speakers, and healers to retreat to places where they can gather their thoughts. Coming inside from the noisy streets of London, and hearing the soothing voice of David Suchet, the audience inside the Cathedral must have had a peace similar to the experience that Jesus and his students felt in their quiet place.

25

2 LISTENING SECTION

Listen to a lecture on the topic you just read about.

3 QUESTION (SUMMARY)

Summarize the points made in the lecture, being sure to explain how the Reading Section deepens the understanding of the lecture passage (150 to 225 words). You have 20 minutes to plan and write your response.

4 LECTURE TRANSCRIPT

David Suchet, famous for acting as Detective Hercule Poirot in the long running television series, is a British actor with a very international background. His parents were of Russian descent. His father had lived in South Africa before moving to London where David Suchet was born in 1946. Suchet was nominated for the highest British film acting award in 1991 for his portrayal of Poirot. He is instantly recognizable in his make-up as the detective: a slightly overweight, middle-aged man perfectly groomed and dressed in a three-piece suit. Poirot speaks English in a heavy French accent and sports a "handlebar" moustache. Some fans are surprised when they see him outside of that role. In real life, Suchet speaks perfectly articulated English, and his face is moustache-free.

5

10

Suchet's biography, *Poirot and Me* gives the details about his being hired for the role. Prior to starring as the detective, he earned a reputation as a serious Shakespearean actor. He joined the Royal Shakespeare Theater in 1973. He starred in such productions as *The Merchant of Venice* and *Macbeth*. He was awarded the Order of the British Empire in recognition of his contribution to the arts.

At first he did not think the Poirot role was suitable for him. He consulted his elder brother about whether he should do it. His brother told him that the Detective Poirot character was rather silly. Nevertheless, Suchet accepted the challenge of making Poirot a serious, deep-thinking character. He added other modern characters to his list of performances. Suchet has portrayed modern people with British, Italian, German and American backgrounds. In 2018, he acted as the fictional Thomas Stanfield, Director of the CIA, in the movie *American Assassin.*

Perhaps one reason for his success is that Suchet is a prolific reader. He has read every one of Agatha Christie's *Poirot* novels. In addition, his much-praised public reading of the entire Gospel of Mark is easily accessible on YouTube. Undoubtedly, he is a man of many talents.

5 BIBLE FOR GLOBAL LITERACY

"He said to them, 'Come away to a deserted place all by yourselves and rest a while.' For many were coming and going, and they had no leisure even to eat." (Mark 6:31 [NRSV])

「イエスは，『さあ，あなたがただけで人里離れた所へ行って，しばらく休むがよい』と言われた。出入りする人が多くて，食事をする暇もなかったからである。」（マルコによる福音書 6 章 31 節）

『マルコによる福音書』は，イエス・キリストの生涯と教えが記されている四つの『福音書』の一つです。聖書に登場する他の多くの名前同様に，著者名の「マルコ」は，英語の "Mark" を始めとして他の西洋の言葉でも非常に多く使われる名前の一つになっています。

　上記の箇所では，イエス・キリストが弟子達に休息を取るようにと敢えて命じています。意外かもしれませんが，休むことを促す教えは聖書の中でも極めて重要な教えの一部となっています。例えば，旧約聖書『創世記』には，神が世界を創造した後に「安息・休息（rest）」されたと記されています。それに倣い，人間も週に一日の「安息日」を守るようにと命じられています。この教えを伝統的に守ってきた西洋（キリスト教）社会の一部では，日曜日にはお店が一斉に閉じられたり，アルコールの販売が制限されたりすることが今でも見られます（ユダヤ教等では土曜日が安息日）。

　21 世紀の現在，人を労働から解放する「安息」の概念は世界でますます重要になってきています。それは，働き方改革の必要が叫ばれる日本だけでなく，労働による抑圧を受けている人々が世界に溢れているからに他なりません。さらに言えば，「安息」が必要なのは人間ばかりではありません。世界のあらゆる生物・自然・環境を人間の搾取から解放することも求められているのではないでしょうか。

6 CULTURAL NOTES

　デイビット・スーシェ氏は，イギリスのミステリーの女王と称されるアガサ・クリスティーの推理小説に登場する探偵エルキュール・ポワロ役で知られる俳優です。この役は多くの俳優が映画でキャスティングされていますが，テレビドラマシリーズ『名探偵ポワロ（原題：Agatha Christie's Poirot)』で 1989 ～ 2013 年の 24 年間，70 話に出演したスーシェ氏が，「原作に最も近いポワロ」と評されています。「灰色の脳細胞」を持つ，几帳面でおしゃれで美食家のベルギー人の名探偵は，第 2 次世界大戦の前，1930 年代のイギリスを舞台に大活躍します。イギリスの田園にそびえる貴

族の館や避暑地のホテルのような華やかな社交界で起こる殺人事件を解決する過程で,「名探偵ポワロ」の独自のスタイルが際立った印象を残します。トレードマークの大きな口ひげを整え,イギリスの未舗装の田舎道を歩くのにもピカピカに磨き上げられたエレガントなエナメルの靴を履き,クレーム・ド・カシスやショコラを好み,時としてフランス語が口をつく,自意識過剰気味のポワロが説得力を持って演じられています。スーシェ氏がイギリス人であることを忘れる名演です。

7 READING SECTION NOTES

l. 1.　feat　偉業

l. 2.　St. Paul's Cathedral　セントポール大聖堂（ロンドンにある英国国教会の聖堂）

l. 3.　distinguished　著名な

l. 4.　Hercule Poirot　エルキュール・ポワロ（アガサ・クリスティの推理小説に登場する私立探偵の名前）

l. 5.　hold someone spellbound　魔法のような力で（人の）心をとりこにする

l. 9.　hoarse　しわがれ声の

l.24.　healer　治療する人

l.24.　retreat to　引きこもる

8 LECTURE NOTES

l. 3.　descent　系統

l. 6.　portrayal of　〜の役柄

l. 7.　perfectly groomed　完璧な身だしなみである

l. 9.　sport　誇示する

l. 9.　handlebar moustache　カイゼル髭（ドイツ皇帝ウィルヘルム二世のように,左右の両側が上にはねあがった八の字のような口髭をさす）

l.11.　articulated　（訛りのない）明瞭に発音された

l.13.　star　（映画や演劇などで）主役を演じる

l.13.　earn a reputation　名声を得る

l.26.　a prolific reader　読書好きな人

9 SUMMARY SAMPLE

David Suchet's international background includes family members with connections to England, South Africa, and Russia. He is British, but the characters he acts include people of American, British, Italian, and German background. He is especially famous for his portrayal as the Belgian detective Hercule Poirot in the longstanding television series. For that role, he dresses in a suit and wears a very recognizable "handlebar" moustache. The character speaks in a heavily French-accented English. In reality, Suchet does not have a moustache, and he speaks English beautifully. He was nominated for acting as Poirot.

Before attracting so much acclaim as "Detective Poirot," Suchet was actually an already celebrated Shakespearean actor. He joined The Royal Shakespeare Theater in the 1970s and performed in such famous plays as *Macbeth* and *The Merchant of Venice*. He is a very versatile actor. When he was offered to do the Poirot role, he asked his brother about it. His brother thought that the Poirot character was rather silly. Nevertheless, Suchet accepted the challenge.

The Lecture mentions David Suchet's perfect English, and the Reading Section notes his beautiful reading. He is an accomplished performer whether he is acting in *Macbeth* on stage, *Hercule Poirot* on television, or reading the *Gospel of Mark* in the Cathedral.

1 READING SECTION

Read the following passage for 3 minutes.

Rick Warren is a pastor of the Saddleback Church in California. He is primarily a Christian preacher, but he is interested in many different things: politics, health, and economics. To him, all of these aspects of life are related. The focus is on helping people make the changes in their lives that will make them more comfortable and productive. He has authored several books which are on the *New York Times* bestseller lists. A recent title is *The Daniel Plan: 40 Days to a Healthier Life.* It is a detailed plan for losing weight. Of course, it emphasizes eating vegetables. His inspiration for the plan comes from a famous Bible story in which ancient Israelites were occupied by a foreign country. Interestingly in that story, the king selected several Israelites for favorable treatment. He even offered his captives rich foods. Daniel, the leader of the favored men, politely declined the choice foods. Instead he requested that he and friends be given "nothing but vegetables to eat and water to drink." At the end of ten days, the young men appeared healthier than others. Daniel was wanting to make a point: God's power would grant them superior health and appearance.

The Daniel Plan has many suggestions on food choices. It also refers to the Bible many times. In keeping with his interest in helping all people (Christians and non-Christians) improve their lives, Warren has a major theme in the book: "... Be transformed by the renewing of your mind."

Simply put, those words mean: we should change our attitudes, and we should think differently. That applies to food addiction as well as to human relationships. Some people are addicted to sugary or fatty foods. If they focus on adding colorful vegetables to their plate, they will be healthier. Similarly, if we decide to spend more time listening to people of other opinions, we might find our circle of friends widening. Certainly, Warren's appeal is not limited to religious people. Government leaders, movie stars, and people coping with medical problems recognize him as a friend.

25

30

2 LISTENING SECTION

Listen to a lecture on the topic you just read about.

3 QUESTION (SUMMARY)

Summarize the points made in the lecture, being sure to explain how the Reading Section deepens the understanding of the lecture passage (150 to 225 words). You have 20 minutes to plan and write your response.

4 LECTURE TRANSCRIPT

Rick Warren is a popular Christian preacher. He was born in California in 1954. He is the founder of the Saddleback Church. Thousands of people crowd into the large auditorium on Sundays to hear him. However, Warren appeals to people of many different interests, not only religion. Recently, he has authored *The Daniel Plan* which is a diet that is drawing world-wide attention. The diet is nearly-vegetarian.

5

Warren might be a good advertisement for his own plan. Once a very heavyset man, he has succeeded in slimming down. Not only has he lost weight, but he has encouraged attendees at his church to emphasize vegetables and minimize meats at their dinners. Movie stars and celebrities are endorsing *The Daniel Plan.* Part of his appeal is humor. He says that he got the idea of the diet during a baptism ceremony at his church. In that ceremony, the preacher must lower people in a pool, then quickly lift them back up. Warren quips that many people on that day were overweight; it strained him to lift them up from the water. Later, at a church service, he asked who would join him in pledging to the diet. Most people accepted his idea.

Warren's influence covers a wide area. He hosted candidates for the United States presidency at a special debate in 2008. Barack Obama, a Democrat, and John McCain, a Republican, presented their ideas at the Forum. He is respected by other world leaders as well. President Paul Kagame of Rwanda invited Warren to conduct a motivational seminar. He has been invited to attend the World Economic Forum in Davos, Switzerland and meetings at Harvard's Kennedy School of Government. He and his wife have launched a campaign to assist people with HIV. Their campaign has two main goals: (1) destigmatize the disease, and (2) offer medical care to patients. Additionally, he has started a treatment program for alcoholics. Warren might be best described as a man interested in helping people change for good.

5 BIBLE FOR GLOBAL LITERACY

"... Be transformed by the renewing of your mind ...." (Romans 12:2 [NIV])

「… 心を新たにして自分を変えていただき …」（ローマの信徒への手紙 12 章 2 節）

　自分という人間を変えるために，まず自分の心を変えるべきと良く言われます。上記の言葉も似ているのですが，違うのは「変えていただき」という部分です。「変える」のは自分の力ではなく，自分よりも大きな存在（神）の力であるというのが上記の言葉なのです。一瞥すると無責任にも思える表現ですが，自分の無力さを認め，自分を変える大きな力があると信じることの大切さは，アルコール依存症から立ち直る 12 ステップといった世界的なプログラムでも広く認められているところです。

　使徒パウロが記した『ローマの信徒への手紙』は，とりわけ西洋（西方）のキリスト教史において極めて重要な役割を果たしてきました。古代キリスト教世界最大の思想家アウグスティヌスは，この書の言葉によって回心に導かれたと言われます。宗教改革者ルターは，この書を通して信仰義認の教えを展開しました。20 世紀最大の神学者と言われるカール・バルトは，彼の時代のキリスト教が人間中心主義に陥っていることに，この書の学びを通して気付かされました。さらに，最近のキリスト教界では，ユダヤ教とキリスト教の関係，教会と国家権力の関係，異文化・異民族交流の問題，また環境問題までもが，この『ローマへの信徒への手紙』を引き合いに出して盛んに議論されています。

6 CULTURAL NOTES

　2013 年に，南カリフォルニアのバプテスト教会の牧師リック・ウォーレンが出版した『**ダニエルプラン：健康な生活への 40 日の道のり**（原題：*The Daniel Plan: 40 Days to a Healthier Life.*）』は，アメリカでベストセラーとなり，今や Web サイトが立ち上がりキリスト教信者以外にも支持され

社会現象となっています。「ダニエル・プラン」は，イスラエルが外国に占領されたときに，囚われたリーダーのダニエルが自分と友人に「野菜と水だけ」を所望し，10日後彼らが他の者たちよりも健康であったという聖書の中の逸話にヒントを得たものです（関連する旧約聖書『ダニエル書』についてはChapter 16の **BIBLE FOR GLOBAL LITERACY** 参照）。基本的に菜食主義を推奨していますが，食べ物だけでなく，生活全般においてより良い選択をすることが大切であるとしています。食事と運動に関することだけでなく，信仰を含めた生き方にも言及しているところが，他のダイエットプランと異なる点です。

　菜食主義（Vegetarian）には多くの種類があります。動物性蛋白質を一切摂らない「ビーガン（Vegan）」や，肉は食べないが魚や卵は食べる「ペスカトリアン（Pescatarian）」など様々なので，ヴェジタリアンの友人と食事をするときは，食べるものと食べないものをあらかじめ聞いておくことをお勧めします。

7 READING SECTION NOTES

l. 1.　pastor　（プロテスタント教会の）牧師

l. 2.　primarily　もともと

l. 2.　preacher　説教者

l.10.　Israelite　（古代）イスラエル（人）の，ユダヤ（人）の現代のイスラエル人はIsraeli

l.12.　captive　捕虜

8 LECTURE NOTES

l. 8.　heavyset　ずんぐりした

l.11.　endorse　（有名人がテレビなどで）宣伝する，支持する

l.19.　Barack Obama　第44代アメリカ合衆国大統領

l.20.　John McCain　2008年アメリカ大統領選共和党候補

l.21.　Paul Kagame　ルワンダ大統領（2000年～）

l.26.　destigmatize　汚名を返上する　　cf. stigmatize 汚名を着せる，de- 接頭辞（否定の意）

9 SUMMARY SAMPLE

Rick Warren is a Christian preacher who influences many people. His church in California has thousands of members. He appeals to people of many different walks of life. The President of Rwanda invited Warren to give a seminar in his country. He has spoken at the World Economic Forum in Davos, Switzerland. American Presidential candidates appeared at a conference which Warren hosted. They debated ideas about how to improve the United States. Warren has also created programs to benefit people suffering from HIV and alcoholism. His recent book, *The Daniel Plan*, is another effort to help people improve their lives. He encourages a near-vegetarian diet. According to the Reading Section, Warren's theme is to encourage people to change their attitudes about food and human relationships.

1 READING SECTION

Read the following passage for 3 minutes.

When Astronaut Buzz Aldrin landed on the moon on Sunday, July 20, 1969, he had a Bible with him. He was an elder of the Presbyterian Church, and he was prepared to observe the Christian ritual of Communion aboard the Apollo lunar module. As he would have done in church, he ate a very small piece of bread and drank a minuscule portion of wine. He read a Bible passage, John 15:5. Neil Armstrong, his fellow astronaut, looked on quietly.

The two men spent 21 hours and 36 minutes at the Tranquility Base landing site. Just before lift-off to return to the earth, Aldrin read yet another Bible passage; this time he read Psalm 8 aloud: "When I consider the work of your (God's) fingers, the moon and the stars which you have set in place, what is man that you are mindful of him?" Psalm 8 was especially suited for Aldrin's moon-surface reading. It mentions the beauty of the moon and the stars. It is a poem of rejoicing. He was quoting the ancient poet, David, who expressed his admiration for the orderliness of the universe. Buzz Aldrin wanted to share his happiness at witnessing stars and moon from such a close vantage point.

It was not the first time that the Bible was carried into space. On December 24, 1968, the Apollo 8 mission orbited the moon. At that time, the crew members took turns reading portions of Genesis, the opening pages of the Bible. The readings were broadcast on earth, angering people who did not believe in God. Madalyn Murray O'Hair, the founder of the American Atheists, sued in the courts. She thought tax-payer money should not be used to honor any religion. She complained to many courts, but ultimately she was not successful in her suits.

2 LISTENING SECTION

Listen to a lecture on the topic you just read about.

3 QUESTION (SUMMARY)

Summarize the points made in the lecture, being sure to explain how the Reading Section deepens the understanding of the lecture passage (125 to 175 words). You have 20 minutes to plan and write your response.

4 LECTURE TRANSCRIPT

Buzz Aldrin, one of the first two men to set foot on the moon, was born in 1930 in New Jersey. Throughout his youth, he demonstrated talent in many areas. As for academics, he earned an "A" average throughout high school. Athletically, he was remarkable as well; he was the starting center football player for Montclair High School. He helped his team in their undefeated 1946 season. They became state champions. Aware of young Aldrin's aptitude, his father enrolled him in the prestigious Severn School, which was attached to the Naval Academy.

After a short time, Aldrin realized that the Navy would not be a good career for him; he suffered seasickness. Further, he had more interest in airplanes than in ships. His father accepted Aldrin's decision to switch to the United States Military Academy in New York. Better known, as West

Point, it is an Army institution. Predictably, Aldrin impressed Army administrators. He earned first place among freshmen students. He also
managed to do well in sports; he was a talented member of the track and
field team. In 1950, he was selected to study American policies in Japan
and the Philippines.

In 1951, as one of the highest ranking graduates of West Point, Aldrin was
given his choice of assignments. He chose to enter the United States Air
Force, which had recently been organized as a separate unit from the Army.
He became an accomplished pilot, eventually flying the most complex
fighter aircraft. He was selected to join the third group of NASA astro-
nauts in 1963. He was the only astronaut at that time to have earned a
doctoral degree. When they landed on the moon in 1969, Buzz Aldrin and
Neil Armstrong became household names. Recently, Aldrin has been cam-
paigning for Americans to explore Mars. To raise money for that event, he
has created a rap music video called *Rocket Experience* with such artists as
Snoop Dogg and Quincy Jones.

5 BIBLE FOR GLOBAL LITERACY

**"When I look at your heavens, the work of your fingers, the moon and the stars
that you have established; what are human beings that you are mindful of them,
mortals that you care for them?" (Psalms 8:3-4 [NRSV])**

「あなたの天を，あなたの指の業を　わたしは仰ぎます。月も，星も，あなたが配置な
さったもの。そのあなたが御心に留めてくださるとは　人間は何ものなのでしょう。人
の子は何ものなのでしょう　あなたが顧みてくださるとは。」（詩編8編4節-5節）

　「あらゆる人は存在しているだけで尊く，その命は全てかけがえのない大切なものである」とい
う聖書の教えが，上記の言葉では詩的に表現されています。
　天・月・星に言及するこの言葉が前提としているのは，世界・宇宙を創造したのは神であるとい
う聖書全体を貫く思想です。神による世界創造という聖書の記述は，科学的な意味における宇宙の
成り立ちを表した言葉というよりも，神という存在の大きさ・崇高さを表すものであると一般に解

釈されています。

　その前提のもとに,「人間の限界・小ささ」と「人間の素晴らしさ・尊さ」,その両方がここで示唆されています。「あなた」とは神のことです。「わたし」は詩編作者であり,人間一般とも言えます。神は,その手で宇宙を創ることができるほど大きな存在であり,より小さな存在である人間は,畏敬の念で神を仰ぐしかないとされます。一方で人間は,その神が「心に留め」,「顧みてくださる」ほどの尊い存在であると記されています。あらゆる人間よりも大きな存在である神が,いと小さき存在でもある人間すべての尊さを認めているということです。

　現代世界は,国家・民族間の紛争に加えて様々な差別や偏見,経済格差の問題を抱えています。全ての人は存在しているだけで尊いという思想は今,ますます意味を持ってきているのではないでしょうか。

6　CULTURAL NOTES

　アポロ 11 号は,NASA のアポロ計画の 5 つ目の有人月面着陸プロジェクトで,ニール・アームストロング船長とバズ・オルドリン月着陸船操縦士の 2 名のアメリカ人が,1969 年 7 月 20 日に人類で初めて,月面着陸を果たしました。アームストロングが月面に最初の一歩を踏み下ろす場面は,テレビ放送を通じて全世界に向けて生中継され,世界の人口の 20 パーセントの人々が,人類が初めて月面を歩く瞬間を見ていたと言われています。アームストロングが「これは一人の人間にとっては小さな一歩だが,人類にとっては偉大な飛躍である」と述べたことはよく知られていますが,バズ・オルドリンが聖書の一節に言及したことは日本人にはあまり知られていないでしょう。オルドリン氏はクリスチャンですが,もしもそうでなくとも,宇宙は人間の小ささと創造主について考え・感じさせられる空間なのだと思います。

7 READING SECTION NOTES

l. 2.   elder of the Presbyterian Church　長老派教会の長老

l. 3.   Christian ritual of Communion　キリスト教の聖餐の儀式

l. 4.   Apollo lunar module　アポロ月着陸船

l. 5.   minuscule　ごくわずかな

l. 8.   Tranquility Base　静かの基地（アポロ11号が着陸した場所）

l.16.   orderliness　整然としていること

l.18.   vantage point　有利な地点

8 LECTURE NOTES

l. 6.   undefeated　全勝の

l.19.   the United States Air Force　アメリカ空軍（略称：USAF）

l.25.   become a household name　有名になる，よく知られるようになる

9 SUMMARY SAMPLE

Buzz Aldrin was multitalented. From his youth he showed a propensity for athletics and academics. He earned "A's" throughout high school while playing on the winning football team. He followed the same pattern at West Point, the Army academy: he was one of the top students, and he participated in track and field sports. Originally, his father planned for him to be in the Navy; however, Aldrin preferred entering the Army where he would not have to worry about seasickness. Also, Aldrin was deeply interested in airplanes, not ships. Around the time of his graduation from West Point, the Air Force was separated from the Army. He decided to join the Air Force where he became a skilled pilot, eventually participating in the Apollo 11 moon landing in 1969. That event, according to the Reading Section, gave Aldrin the opportunity to acknowledge his faith. He read the Bible twice from the capsule on that mission. Aldrin was academic, athletic and spiritual.

著者紹介

Harris G. Ives（ハリス G. アイヴス）
　担当箇所：READING SECTION, LISTENING SECTION
　　　　　　SUMMARY, CHRISTIANITY AROUND YOU
　専門分野：アメリカ文学
　茨城キリスト教大学名誉教授

上野　尚美（うえの　なおみ）
　担当箇所：READING SECTION & LISTENING
　　　　　　SECTION NOTES、編集全般
　専門分野：英語教育学
　茨城キリスト教大学教授

村上　美保子（むらかみ　みほこ）
　担当箇所：CULTURAL NOTES
　専門分野：英語教育学、応用言語学
　茨城キリスト教大学教授

小幡　幸和（おばた　ゆきかず）
　担当箇所：BIBLE FOR GLOBAL LITERACY
　専門分野：世界キリスト教学
　茨城キリスト教大学准教授

イラスト　　佃彰一郎

聖書を引用する世界の著名人
── TOEFL iBT 形式で学ぶ英語とグローバルリテラシー ──

著作者	Harris G. Ives・上野尚美・村上美保子・小幡幸和
	© 学校法人茨城キリスト教学園
発行者	武村哲司
印刷所	日之出印刷株式会社

2021 年 2 月 22 日　第 1 版第 1 刷発行

発行所　　株式会社　開拓社	〒112-0013　東京都文京区音羽 1-22-16
	電話　（03）5395-7101（代表）
	振替　00160-8-39587
	http://www.kaitakusha.co.jp

ISBN978-4-7589-2313-2　C0082